MW01034634

From Atheism to
Catholicism

How Scientists
and Philosophers
Led Me to Truth

Kevin Vost

Our Sunday Visitor Publishing Division
Our Sunday Visitor, Inc.
Huntington, Indiana 46750

From Atheism to
Catholicism

Acknowledgments

In early January 2009, Michael Dubruiel suggested I submit this book idea to Bert Ghezzi at Our Sunday Visitor. I was able to thank Michael before his unexpected death. Now I also thank Bert, and I thank God for guiding me to both of them.

CONTENTS

God Bless the Atheists

*"Yet closer scrutiny shows that even in the philosophical think-
ing of those who helped drive faith and reason further apart
there are found at times precious and seminal insights which,
if pursued and developed with mind and heart rightly tuned,
can lead to the discovery of truth's way."*

POPE JOHN PAUL II, *Fides et Ratio*[1]

"Way to a Christian virtue. *Learning from one's enemies is
the best way toward loving them; for it makes us grateful to
them."*

FRIEDRICH NIETZSCHE, *Mixed Opinions and Maxims*[2]

Bless those who persecute you.

ROMANS 12:14

This book is a story of the interaction between the individuals and ideas that led me toward God, away from Him,
and back to Him to stay. It's certainly not all about me though.
Many young people in today's world are led astray from their
faith by atheistic philosophies, psychologies, and even biolo-
gies. However, my goal is *not* to parry with, put down, pon-
tificate to, beat up, belittle, besmirch, or otherwise pommel or
befuddle any classical or modern-day atheists. Instead, I'd like
to highlight, at least at first, what they've got going for them,
the exciting ideas and partial truths in their systems of thought

that can inspire their youthful adherents to abandon the faith of their fathers. It is heady stuff, after all, to think oneself a "superman" (or "superwoman"), one of the superior ones who has broken the chains of ancient superstition and stands ready to forge a brave new world of the future.

My plan is to start by giving you my take on a handful of atheistic philosophers who inspired me in my youth. This comprises "Part I: God Is Dead?" We'll address notable atheists including the philosophers Friedrich Nietzsche, Bertrand Russell, and Ayn Rand, and the agnostic psychologist Albert Ellis — not to mention the current prince of the "new atheists" and "Darwin's bulldog," biologist Richard Dawkins. These are folks who taught, or still teach, that faith and reason go together like oil and water, or as Rand once put it, like poison and food! I'll highlight their most innovative ideas, what I drew from them, and in some cases, even their opinions of each other. As proud and cantankerous as they could be, these folks were the intellectual company I kept during my own 20s and 30s.

In "Part II: Signs of Life," we'll look at some psychologists and philosophers, including Alfred Adler (the namesake of my doctoral alma mater), and the great Greek and Roman Stoics, who, though certainly as profound as the "Part I" folks, did not necessarily believe that reason rules out belief in God, and who provided me, and all of us, with some handy and useful guides to good living. They point us on our way.

In "Part III: Christ Has Risen From His Tomb!" we'll look to the folks who brought me back home to Athens, Jerusalem, and Rome. Here we will look at true intellectual giants, men who knew that knowledge and reason did not begin on earth when they developed their own higher thinking abilities during their own adolescence. Here we will see thinkers who know that faith and reason are much more like vinegar and oil than like oil and water. We'll see how they move from "the god of the philosophers" to "the God of Abraham, Isaac, and Jacob." I'll start with St. Thomas Aquinas in the 13th century, work through two giants of the 20th century — C. S. Lewis and G. K. Chesterton — and end with a man whose funeral I myself attended in April 2005. After all, it was he, in his famous letter *Fides et Ratio* (Faith and Reason), who told us (see the quotation at the beginning of this chapter) that by carefully examining the ideas of those who worked to drive faith and reason apart, we may be led to the truth. And even Nietzsche saw the sense in learning from one's enemies.

Still, I don't want to think of these people as enemies if they and their followers are serious seekers of the truth. I wouldn't ask God to damn the atheists, as much as to bless them. Indeed, I once saw Ayn Rand herself, someone not particularly known for Christian charity, willing to say "God bless you" on *The Phil Donahue Show*! If someone believes that truth matters, there is always hope while he is alive that he will someday open his heart to Him who is Truth. Further, we will be far more likely to open hearts if we can show people that we have heard what they've had to say. There's an old saying that "a man convinced against his will is a man of the same opinion still." I don't want to try to twist anybody's will behind his back. My hope is simply that some who have been drawn to atheism might be willing to listen to some good old-fashioned theism as well.

So, if you'll allow me a couple of autobiographical pages to set the stage, soon I'll fill it up with some of the superstars of atheism in Part I of our story.

Was Superman a Catholic?

You'll see in the Introduction that I was a "Supermanian" from way back, but I also grew up Catholic. Every Sunday we went to Mass, then out for a big breakfast (and often to a toy store) as well. Monday through Friday were spent with my friends and the Dominican sisters of dear old one-classroom-per-grade, established in 1912, St. Agnes School of Springfield, Illinois. At home, however, we didn't pray together, read the Bible, or talk much about God at all. Dad, a convert from Methodism for the sake of my Irish Catholic mother, never spoke about religious matters. I was always proud to see him, though, when he was called upon at church to usher and go down the aisles with one of those old collection-baskets-on-a-stick. Dad, a plasterer by trade, was tough, incredibly hardworking, and despite some innate orneriness, often quite self-sacrificing for the family. Mom didn't talk religion either, but she sure embodied true Christian goodness and kindness to her children.

So, I grew up as a Catholic-educated, Mass-going, altar-serving, nominal Catholic. It was in my sophomore year in a Catholic high school when those abstract and hypothetical (*if-then*) thinking abilities of adolescence started to bloom. It occurred to me that *if* all this "Jesus stuff" was true, *then* truly, it is the most important "stuff" in all the world and I really should try to live by it. Hence followed a couple of years of absorption in the Bible and the Church, in an attempt to walk the talk and live the faith.

These years were the mid-1970s, and there were quite a few "saved" and "born-again" teens and young adults roaming about in central Illinois at the time. A couple of weightlifting buddies — one a former Catholic — were going to the same Bible-based Pentecostal church in town, and I often went along. Many of these young people had no serious religious commitment before they were "saved." Some were former drug addicts or delinquent ne'er-do-wells of various stripes. They seemed very genuinely changed, though. Some would wince or shake their heads a bit when I told them I was Catholic, since to them it meant I was not "Christian." Still, though rather ecumenically-minded, I remained quite happy in the Catholic

Church. I enjoyed the works of Billy Graham and other authors available at the local "Christian" bookstore. I watched the ill-fated *PTL Club*, and the *700 Club* as well. I knew for a fact, though, that the Catholic Church had Jesus too, and we also had Archbishop Fulton J. Sheen!

A friend of my mom's at the time was a charismatic Catholic, and though our personalities just didn't jibe so well (and Mom remained more Christian in her ethical behavior than in her overt acts of religion), I knew that her friend's faith in Christ was just as real as any of my Bible-alone brethren. One friend had left the Church and converted to Protestantism. I respected my born-again friends and enjoyed sharing in Christ with them, but I never felt the slightest urge to leave the Catholic Church for any other manner of Christianity. Indeed, at one point during my freshman year of college, I met with a seminarian from our parish as I tried to discern a possible vocation to the priesthood, which was not to be my call. (Oddly enough, my own reading during my teen years consisted primarily of a combination of muscle magazine articles and religious books.)

Just a short time later, still in my freshman college year, I was back to that darn hypothetical *if-then* thinking. The *then*, of course, depends on the *if.* The conclusion depends on the starting presumptions. Not through any college course, but through my own burgeoning love of books and ideas, I discovered the world of the worldly philosophers, such as Friedrich Nietzsche and his bold superman; the ever brilliant, witty, and excitingly hedonistic Bertrand Russell; and the exotically different, heroically triumphant, and unabashedly vocal Ayn Rand. And believe it or not, this also tied in to those darn muscle magazines, of all things, as the reigning 1978 Mr. Universe — one brilliant young man by the name of Mike Mentzer — was challenging the dogmas of the bodybuilding world and promoting the philosophical ideas of Nietzsche, and later Ayn Rand, to boot!

There is an old saying that "a little philosophy leads to atheism," and lo, there was I led. The *truth* of my *if* had been taken away. I had come to reason that *if* all this Jesus stuff is *not* true, *then* it is *not important* and *I should not be living my life by it!* And to some extent, there I stayed for more than 20 years, after more than a little philosophy, and a master's degree and doctorate in psychology as well.

Before I move on, let me note that I did not intend this section heading as purely a teaser. Was Superman a Catholic, or at least some form of Christian? I don't really recall Superman's religion being addressed in the TV shows and movies I have watched. Still, others before me have pointed to interesting facts like these:

- The comic book "Man of Steel" was not of this earth, was raised by human foster parents, slowly came into his full powers, started his good works in young adulthood, championed the good, and had both "truth" and the "way" in his most famous motto.
- People did not realize who he truly was, and he relentlessly fought against evil.
- In the novel *The Death and Life of Superman*,[3] he spends time in a tomb, people later find it empty, and he is seen again on earth, but in an altered form.

Wherever do these writers get their storylines?

A Scholarly Tome on the Philosophy of Atheism (or What This Book Is *Not*)

As we consider the writings of the great atheistic and agnostic philosophers, psychologists, and biologists, we will have no choice at times but to sail into some very deep and treacherous philosophical waters. Things like existence and being, axioms and proofs, rationalism and empiricism, probabilities and intelligent design, free will and determinism, hedonism and utilitarianism, and selves and "memes" may threaten our voyage like Scylla and Charybdis. (For those unfamiliar with these fabled monsters making difficult a narrow passage through ancient Mediterranean waters, you may substitute "a rock and a hard place.") But don't worry: one advantage of the great theistic thinkers I have encountered is their ability to cut through the jargon and make those murky waters much more fathomable. I will neither intend nor pretend to soundly refute the arguments of any militant atheist. I will merely strive to present the arguments in such a way that the average reader can obtain a gist of what is being spoken about, and a glimpse of how the great theists make the issues so clear and understandable.

So, when I talk about abstract issues or use philosophical jargon, be aware that I will be doing my darnedest to render it amenable to common sense, that basic capacity that the great atheists and theists, and that you and I, share in the simple fact of our humanity, made as we are in the image of God — if I might interject such a point so early on in the book!

I also make no claims regarding this book's inclusiveness. There are all sorts of interesting atheistic, agnostic, and theistic thinkers out there, of course, but my readers will have to settle for the ones who interested me. All in all, then, if you are looking for a meticulously researched, irrefutably reasoned, carefully qualified, copiously quantified, and fully footnoted tome on the history and philosophy of atheism, please set this slim guide aside and seek elsewhere for a heftier, dustier tome. I'll tell you next what *is* in this one.

Recollections and Reflections
(or What this Book *Is*)

Here lies my goal for the chapters ahead. As I noted before, I want to show readers who and what led me toward atheism and away from faith, and how they set the stage for a much deeper return to faith — without abandonment of reason — more than 20 years later. Still, I intend to present much more than one particular "reversion story," as I hope to address issues that have pulled millions from the path toward God, not all of whom have returned.

When we reach Chapter 6, on psychological theorist Alfred Adler, I'm going to fill you in on his psychological theory of "early recollections," an idea that I find most valuable. Briefly, for now, Adler holds that our handful of memories from earliest childhood tells a world about who we are today. Of all the myriad of experiences in our lives, that small selection that we retain for a lifetime has served an important purpose in forming who we are, or else we would have forgotten those experiences in favor of others.

Here is how the concept "recollections" fits into this book. As I type away at the keys during my 48th year, I will be combing my mind for my own early recollections, not only from early childhood but also from my mid-teens, when immersed in Christianity, to my late teens, when I turned to atheism, all the way to my early 40s, when my journey brought me back home to Christ and His Church. In the spirit of Adler and his recollection theory, my own recollections of the great atheists and agnostics will provide the basis of my story. I spent years immersed in the writings of some, especially Ayn Rand and Albert Ellis, and had read at least a handful of books by the others.

What I will endeavor to do, then, is to write primarily from the resources of my own memory. Now, those who know me as the author of a book on memory techniques might suspect this is kind of like cheating, but these are not the kinds of lessons that I sat down and tried to *formally* memorize! These are the lessons that I read and reread and then went on to live. This approach should also help keep me from getting a little too pedantic and reverting too much to my professorial role. I don't see your name on the roll call for my lecture course, after all!

Still, I believe in accuracy, and I will dip into my library to pull forth some direct quotations and to re-immerse myself to some extent in those worlds that so captivated me in my youth. I will also show that I've become familiar with the works of the most recent atheists, and with their theistic counterparts as well.

As I first decided to do this, there was that little, but lingering, thought that perhaps I would be so struck by some of these folks' ideas after returning to them (there's the "reflections" part of this section heading) that maybe my faith would stand a little shaken. You'll soon see for yourself if that came to pass.

One more thing that has become increasingly clear — and amazing — to me is that all the time I spent studying things either directly opposed to or apparently neutral regarding God and His Church was laying the groundwork for future works to His glory. My study of memory techniques would lead to a book on memorizing *the faith*. My years immersed in fitness training would lead to a book on physical *and spiritual* fitness. My years immersed in learning about Aristotelian and Stoic virtues would lead to a book proclaiming *Christian* virtues. And now, my years of immersion in atheistic philosophy has led to the modest volume you hold in your hands. *Ad majorem Dei gloriam!*[4]

Truth Boxes

Here's another feature of this book. Have you ever heard what Nietzsche considered the most profound statement in the entire Bible? It was mouthed by Roman curator Pontius Pilate. I refer you to John 18:38 — "What is truth?" While I take issue with Nietzsche's opinion on the relative greatness of scriptural passages, I think he is correct that Pilate's question is a very, very important one. That's why, as a special feature at the end of each chapter, I will include a special "truth box."

In Part I, on the atheists, these boxes will primarily consider "untruths." While a considerable portion of these chapters will focus on what is good in their systems, what appealed to me, and what draws in other adherents, these truth boxes will point out some chinks in the armor of these thinkers who would dare enjoin battle with God. I will question their questions, and raise doubts about their doubts. These will, in turn, be addressed and answered in the chapters that follow. The truth boxes for the theistic thinkers in Part II will consider partial truths, and those for the Christian theologians and philosophers of Part III will consider full truths. The concluding truth box will be entitled "The Words of the Word."

Now let's get down to business. We wouldn't want to keep Superman waiting.

Neither Bird, nor Plane,
but Superman!

"I teach you the [superman]. *Man is something that shall be overcome. What have you done to overcome him?*"

Friedrich Nietzsche[1]

"It is not at all necessary first to inoculate man with the desire to develop into superman, as the daring attempt of Nietzsche has maintained.... The origin of humanity and the ever-repeated beginning of infant life impresses with every psychological act: 'Achieve! Arise! Conquer!'... The striving for perfection is innate as something which belongs to life, a striving, an urge, a developing, a something without which one could not even conceive of life."

Alfred Adler[2]

"Truth, Justice, and the American Way!"

Superman

Let me set the stage: Our nation is at war with communism in Vietnam, and with our own traditional political, economic, religious, ethical, and sexual principles, right here within the U.S.A. Everything is in turmoil and turning upside down. The 1950s are over. *Leave It to Beaver* has left and *Father* (no longer) *Knows Best*. Paul VI is pope, Lyndon Johnson is president, but I hardly know or care because it is 1967, I am only 6 years old, and I'm busy being happily mesmerized by the most amazingly awesome being I have ever seen or imagined.

Flying there on the TV screen, it's not a bird, nor a plane. Of course not — it's Superman! He stands out from the crowd in his audaciously unusual blue, red, and yellow outfit, proud "S" upon his chest, cape and all. He stops trains, leaps buildings, and bullets bounce off him. Women adore him. Good men look up to him. Yet this guy is incredibly humble. He takes little credit for his endless string of good and daring deeds. He doesn't even want people to know who he really is. All he wants is to expend his superhuman and unearthly powers for "Truth, Justice, and the American Way!"

Like many young lads, then and now, I lived and breathed Superman in those halcyon days of youth. We still have a few old photos of me in my Superman costume, with completely duct-taped knees from overuse, striking solemn poses, surely preparing to do good and fight evil over some issue I can no longer recall. My dear mother used to laugh and say that her friends called her "Superman's Mom."

Mom also fondly told the story of one time our family went to a wedding. I was told that I could not dress as Superman there. Fortunately, for me, I was able to persuade an older cousin to take me out to the car (which was to serve as my makeshift phone booth). Soon after, a young Superman sat down in the pew with his mortified mother. Dad was amused. I never once remember him discouraging my Superman enthusiasm. And to tell you the truth, Mom got a kick out of it, too. She passed this all along to my wife, and my wife to her friends and mine.

That is why, as I type, I sip from a Superman mug. I sometimes wear my Superman pajamas, write with Superman pens, eat from a Superman place mat, put Superman stickers on my cards to friends, have (or have had) a Superman lunch pail, key chain, T-shirts, sweatshirt, slippers, birthday cake, cookies, Christmas ornaments — you name it, and almost anything that can be Superman-ized has been given to me. Just this last year, rascally friends from work gave me a small box with the alluring label of "New Ronco Super Pecs Booster" on the outside, only to hold a small green stone labeled "Ha! Kryptonite" on the inside.

All right, back to 1967 and "truth, justice, and the American way." I didn't realize it at the time, but in the 1960s we were really starting to question if there was such a thing as "the American way" — or even "truth" and "justice," come to think of it. I'll address that a little later. For now, let me explain why I'm starting a book on theology for atheists and theists that features "The Man of Steel."

Because my formal educational background is in psychology, I am going to approach the issues of atheism and theism partly from a psychological perspective. I will appeal to both the psychology of the *idiopathic* (individual) *differences*, how we each have our own unique personalities and histories (with Superman playing a big role in mine early on), and of the *nomothetic* (common) *elements* of human psychology shared by all. I will argue that Superman (or some equivalent) plays a large role in the psychology of all of us (and ultimately points us toward God), whether from the get-go, or after decades of struggle in adulthood.

Another thing about my own psychology is a deep interest in things philosophical and, more recently, theological. I will be addressing here systems of philosophy, one of which even popularized the term "superman" and another which explicitly praised the concept of superheroes and stated its goal as making man a hero.

At some level, in our childhood years we all strive to be more than what we are, to become the most powerful and best versions of ourselves. In this culture, superheroes often serve as such models. This is especially true for boys, though there are some equivalents for girls, such as Wonder Woman and She-Ra. As we grow just a little older, of course, we realize that there really is no Superman, like there really is no Santa Claus. Many of us may even become sophisticated enough to "realize" that neither is there a God. Quite interestingly, some highly intelligent philosophers and scientists who come to see belief in God as the folly of the ignorant actually retain a belief in a superman. This is not the Superman of the comics, of course, but the superman of the philosophers. I speak of Nietzsche and others influenced strongly by theories of evolution and speculation about where it may be leading us. (We'll see in the pages ahead how this superman's kryptonite is truth.)

Others, retaining a heroic ideal while rejecting both God and evolution (e.g., Ayn Rand and the Objectivists), paint man himself as the ultimate hero. Still others — and actually, most of the current crop of atheist thinkers who see the world through the lenses of biology, rather than philosophy — have indeed dropped the superman as well. They would not have us look to something higher, but would reduce us to the same plane as any other animal — Lord (and Superman), help us!

But I'll submit from the beginning that there is still much we can learn from Superman and "the superman" — and from Santa Claus and St. Nicholas for that matter. Indeed, by rationally examining the theories of the atheists, we can find that there really is a God. Indeed, we could even say that His reality far surpasses that of our own! (I'll explain in due course.)

Let me conclude this introduction by noting that one conception of the "superman," an idea put forth by some as an alternative to Christian belief, can actually help lead us to Christ. So, when things get a little philosophically or theologically heavy, bear in mind that "The Man of Steel" may stop by from time to time to keep things light for us, acting much like a beefed-up, modern-day Simon of Cyrene, helping us bear our burdens along this all-important intellectual and spiritual journey toward God.

Enough said. Let's move up and away from the Introduction and see what this book is really all about.

PART I

God Is Dead?

"For the old Gods came to an end long ago. And verily it was a good and joyful end of Gods!

"They did not die lingering in the twilight — although that lie is told! On the contrary, they once upon a time — laughed themselves to death!

"That came to pass when, by a God himself, the most ungodly word was uttered, the word: 'There is but one God! Thou shalt have no other gods before me.' "

FRIEDRICH NIETZSCHE, *Thus Spoke Zarathustra*[1]

CHAPTER 1

Friedrich Nietzsche's Superman

*"All beings so far have created something beyond themselves;
and do you want to be the ebb of this great flood and even go
back to the beasts rather than overcome man? What is the ape
to man? A laughingstock or a painful embarrassment. And
man shall be just that for the superman: a laughingstock or a
painful embarrassment...."*
FRIEDRICH NIETZSCHE, *Thus Spoke Zarathustra*[1]

"Dead are all Gods: now we will that superman live...."
FRIEDRICH NIETZSCHE, *Thus Spoke Zarathustra*[2]

Two mighty mustachioed musclemen emerged from their
war chariot, eyes poised on the sack of Troy. The elder, like
a wizened Agamemnon, had come to extend his empire; the
younger, like a powerful Achilles, fated to live a short, but glorious life, stood ready to take on all who would test his mettle.
A sea of stalwart warriors parted in awe as the king and his
champion prepared to claim their prize.

All right, so I've exaggerated a bit. The chariot was really a taxi cab, and the city was not Troy, but St. Louis, Mis-
souri. The scene took place not in 1200 B.C. but in A.D. 1978.
And the first of the two mustachioed musclemen was actually
Joe Weider, president of Weider Enterprises and publisher of
Muscle & Fitness magazine, brother to Ben Weider, president of
the International Federation of Bodybuilders (IFBB), the man

who brought future California governor Arnold Schwarzenegger to America, and the self-proclaimed "Trainer of Champions since 1936!" The younger man was actually Mike Mentzer, the reigning Mr. Universe (the first ever to obtain a perfect score) and the latest and greatest of his trainer's champions.

So what does this have to do with Nietzsche? I pray you'll forgive me my digressions, but I'm really not too far off course. It was through that young, mustachioed Achilles, Mike Mentzer, that I would come to know another fierce, mustachioed warrior, not of the body, but of the mind: Friedrich Nietzsche.

You see, Weider and Mentzer had come to St. Louis for a joint powerlifting and bodybuilding contest, held in conjunction with a meeting to explore the merging of the two major governing bodies of bodybuilding competition, the aforementioned IFBB and the AAU (Amateur Athletic Union). Mentzer himself had come to provide a posing exhibition of his superhuman physique and to conduct a bodybuilding seminar the next day. Ken Waller, a St. Louis native and former Mr. Universe himself, had introduced Mentzer by saying that to see this much muscle at one place in St. Louis, you'd have to go visit Phil, the St. Louis Zoo's most famous gorilla!

Mentzer was impressive all right, displaying his thick and powerful physique to the strains of *Siegfried's Funeral March* by Wagner. He impressed me much more the next day, however, at the seminar. Mentzer, you see, saw himself as a bit of an iconoclast — one who shatters idols with the hammer of the truth. He emerged from that cab with Weider — his editor, benefactor, and boss — but he informed us in the seminar to be skeptical of what we read in the muscle magazines, since they were actually registered as catalogs, and existed mostly to sell products.

Mentzer was that rare phenomenon of "the thinking man's bodybuilder." He had actually studied college texts of physiology and nutrition, and had participated in medical research on exercise and fitness. And not only did he smash idols, but he also burst a few of the bubbles in the minds of his seminar audience.

Back in the 1970s, we teenage muscleheads were assured that if we consumed enough protein and vitamin supplements and trained like Arnold Schwarzenegger (up to twice daily), we, too, could look like him. Mentzer, however, had the temerity to tell us about our inborn genetic limitations, that the key to being a world-class bodybuilder was "choosing the right parents," that protein supplements could not force our muscles to grow (but could produce a lot of unwanted fat), and that if Arnold knew the best way to train, "then why aren't there thousands of Arnolds running around?"

Mentzer preached a fitness message of brief, intense, infrequent strength training and a simple commonsense diet of normal food that has worked for me for more than 30 years after that fateful seminar. In fact, I wrote all about it in *Fit for Eternal Life*. But Mentzer also preached a philosophy or worldview in his writings that has continued to affect me as well, though I have discarded important parts of it. Mentzer, you see, had a curious and probing philosophical mind. Mentzer was an iconsmasher in the world of bodybuilding. Nietzsche thought that he had smashed the very gods (and God) the icons represented. Let's move on, then, to examine that fiercely strange philosopher, as muscular in mind as Mentzer was in body.

Preacher, Saint, and Antichrist

Nietzsche was a strange, murky, mysterious figure to me in my youth. He'd been associated with the beyond-good-and-evil power politics of G. Gordon Liddy. A school friend had told me an anecdote of dubious veracity of a scantily-clad woman of ill-repute reading from the works of Nietzsche on the streets of

New Orleans. And here was Mike Mentzer, the muscular guru of my teens, writing about Nietzsche within the pages of my sacred muscle magazines and within his own books.

Now, I don't believe it was Nietzsche who pulled me from my faith. I was doing a lot of reading at the time, including the works of the other folks who appear in Part I of this book, and I do not recall any particular "Aha!" experience that made my faith disappear. The philosopher of the *ubermench* (superman) was surely among those early atheistic influences, though. And I do recall that after Mentzer, my first knowledge of Nietzsche came through historian Will Durant's *The Story of Philosophy* — and what an intriguing character he was!

Born in Prussia, on October 15, 1844, the son of a Lutheran minister who would die when young Friedrich was but 4 years old, the man who would later declare God had died was known by his young peers as "the little preacher." He could reportedly bring tears to listeners' eyes with his reading of Scripture. He was also quite strong-willed as a child and a devotee of the classic literature of the ancient Greeks and Romans. He had read the story of the Roman Mutius Scaevola, who struck fear in the heart of the enemies of Rome by calmly holding a burning coal in his right hand until his hand was destroyed.[3] When young friends scoffed at this story, young Nietzsche held lit matches in his own hand to demonstrate.

Nietzsche remained devoted to those Greco-Roman classics, becoming a philologist and writing books on the key themes of the literature and philosophy of the Greeks. His Christian devotion, however, waned, to understate things just a bit. In his later days, he wrote a book called *The Antichrist*, and when he had become insane, used this label for himself. Ironically, after he died in 1900, local inhabitants referred to the personally unobtrusive philosopher as "the saint."

Conan the Philosopher: Nietzsche's Powerful Appeal to the Adolescent Male Mind

Almost any adult who has survived adolescence will nod in quiet assent to modern psychologists' descriptions of "adolescent egocentrism." Teens develop higher abstract reasoning powers — including the ability to imagine and reason through all kinds of hypothetical "if-then" or "what-if" situations — yet they have little experience to help them see the limitations of their ponderings. This may lead them to the questioning of all sorts of things they've been taught, not to mention those who have taught them. Mark Twain once summed it up by saying that when he was 14 his father was so ignorant that he could hardly stand him, but by age 21 he was amazed at what his dad had learned in only seven years!

Typical results of the adolescent's new untested thinking powers include what modern psychologist David Elkind[4] calls the *"personal fable,"* the idea that one's own destiny is special and unique (which, in a sense, it certainly is), but more unique than that of others. Common to this feeling is a sense that others just cannot understand you and also a *"sense of invincibility,"* a feeling that one is specially protected and invulnerable to harm, which may lead to the risky behaviors so often associated with the teen years. Further, the teen may experience the sense of an *"imaginary audience,"* or a feeling that all eyes are focused on him.

The intoxicating world of the Nietzschean superman meshes quite nicely with all of these features of adolescent *egocentrism* (self-centered thinking). Nietzsche would have us question all traditions — and turn many upside down. He projected his own incredible fable — not merely a personal fable, but a super-personal fable! Nietzsche saw his own unique destiny as that of a prophet who would overturn the meek and slavish morality of Christianity and replace it with one more bold, daring, and vibrant (though more cold, uncaring, and violent as well). He saw as man's highest calling, not his capacity to seek good and avoid evil, but his will to seek power to satisfy his desires. Indeed, one of his books was entitled *Beyond Good and Evil*. This capacity of man to attain and display the power to obtain whatever he pursues, unaffected by traditional moral restraints, would be best displayed in the magnificent superman to follow us.

As we see, Nietzsche projected not just an ideal man, but also a creature who will be embarrassed even to think he arose from man. In Chapter 6, we'll examine the theories of Alfred Adler, who himself was influenced, in part, by Nietzsche. Adler wrote of the *"inferiority complex,"* an exaggerated sense of one's own weakness, which, if severe enough, will sometimes give rise to a *"superiority complex,"* complete with a tendency to *"overcompensate"* for those feelings of weakness by acting as if one felt strong — stronger, indeed, than his fellow man. It seems quite likely that Nietzsche's superman developed from the philosopher's own superiority complex. He felt small, but he fantasized big! Perhaps, then, the bold, daring superman of the future arose from the insecurities of the reserved, timid philosopher of Nietzsche's own present. And speaking of a sense of invincibility, nobody messes with the superman!

Nietzsche's early descriptions of the superman, his replacement for a "dead" God, suggest a more highly evolved creature of the future, yet he later made it clear that the attainment of the superman was not a matter of letting nature take its course. Rather, it called for "eugenics," for careful and purposeful breeding of the greatest, strongest, and boldest, coupled with highly disciplined upbringing and education. The superman will not just happen. We are called to pave the way for him by rejecting the values of Christianity, democracy, and any creed or system of belief that would hinder the great man in his exercise of power and dominance over the great herd of lesser men.

As for the adolescent "imagined audience," Nietzsche's own actual audience of readers was really quite small in his lifetime. He had to pay to have the first edition of *Thus Spoke Zarathustra* published, and it sold only 40 copies. He imagined a much vaster audience of future readers, though, and in this he was correct.

Add now to this mixture of egocentric thinking tendencies, an XY chromosomal pairing in his adolescent reader (i.e., that he is a male brimming over with testosterone), and you have an ideal follower of Nietzsche and his particular non-comic version of Superman. How he loves to boldly defy. What an "in your face" philosopher he is. He is Conan the Philosopher! He stands ready to sing of will and power and dominance and lust, and to do so in very well-turned, memorable, and sometimes quite humorous (if one does not take them seriously) aphorisms and catchphrases.

Nietzsche teaches the young man (in pretty close paraphrase of his *Thus Spoke Zarathustra*[5]) that that which does not kill him will make him stronger; that man is for war and woman for the recreation of the warrior; that pity is for the weak; that sex, the lust to rule, and selfishness are things the real man seeks; that the highest good is to be brave; and that that which is half-and-half spoils the whole.

Note well Nietzsche's praise of strength and lust and dominance and power. He takes those powerful urges and feelings that society tells a young man to temper and control and then encourages him to unleash them. The follower of Nietzsche, therefore, can express his lower animal nature to make way for the higher superman of the future, feeling disdain for those too weak, dull, and timid to face this Nietzschean liberation along the way.

Nietzsche also writes that a day is lost if we haven't danced once; that a truth is false if not accompanied by a laugh; that his crude language is for the people, because he speaks not for "Angora rabbits, ink-fish or pen-hacks";[6] that he spits "on cities of compressed souls and narrow chests";[7] that he mocks the winter with a cold bath; that churches are but huts or sweet-smelling caves that men build; that women are incapable of friendship, being still cats and birds, "or at best, cows"[8] — yet, as one biographer notes, "even a superman may have a taste for beautiful ankles."[9]

Here we see Nietzsche proclaiming that the path of the superman will be marked by great joy in living, by dancing and laughter and carefree use of women — though he later argues for carefully controlled "eugenics" for breeding of the superman. Nietzsche then speaks to youth in their own language, urging them, in essence, to "question authority," and telling them decades before the hippies: "If it feels good, do it!"

Nietzsche is often like the ornery little toddler who says something or does something naughty, and if you're not personally offended or insulted, you just can't help but smile — and he knows it! The problem is that he has made attacks on very important things like Christianity, Christian virtue, and the dignity of women, and many have taken him seriously, all too seriously. Others have interpreted and misinterpreted his ideas in support of causes as heinous as that of the Nazis, who saw the blond-beast they would usher in as the superior race of super men and women.

Not intending an *ad hominem* argument to invalidate his philosophy itself, I cannot help but point out that Nietzsche himself was neither a bold blond giant, a fearless warrior, nor any kind of heavily-muscled Mr. Universe contender. This champion of "life as war" served as a medic in a real war — certainly an extremely honorable role, but not exactly Nietzschean:

Why coddle the weak and afflicted, after all? This champion of lust and the "well-turned ankle" was apparently quite chaste, having lost the woman of his desires to another contemporary philosopher of little repute today. Finally, this despiser of weakness and enemy of pity would spend the last years of his life insane, cared for by his loving Christian sister, until his death in 1900.

The *Ubermench* and Me

I never really considered myself a Nietzschean, though his ideas did intrigue, inspire, and amuse me in my late teens. As I flip through my copy of Penguin Books' *The Portable Nietzsche* (Walter Kauffman translation), I see dozens… no, hundreds of passages still brightly marked with yellow highlighter from the 1970s.[10]

Just now, I've returned from my closet with an old T-shirt. There, emblazoned upon a calm, baby-blue background is the intense and mustachioed mien of Friedrich Nietzsche himself. When I was a competitive powerlifter back in the early '80s, partly because of my own association of Nietzsche with that living, physical "superman" — Mr. Universe, Mike Mentzer — the image of Nietzsche actually gave fire and intensity to my strength-training workouts. Coupled with some pre-workout Wagnerian music[11] and mugs of coffee strong enough to set an elephant on its ear,[12] I was inspired to endure whatever pain and effort it took to build my muscles to "supermanian" proportions. I really don't know if I'd have ever squatted over 500 pounds without Nietzsche and Mentzer! My limited understanding of Nietzsche's philosophy at that time helped me feel big, bold, and strong. I did not understand at that time how his philosophy of exaggeration and excess overshot the balanced "golden mean"[13] of a purposeful, controlled, and directed sense of strength and courage that characterizes true manliness.

The contents of Nietzsche's ideas have influenced many important thinkers. Freud, Adler, and many other psychologists were to borrow from Nietzsche — for example, his emphasis on the force that unconscious drives for power and sex can play in the determination of our behaviors.[14]And as for his writing style, Nietzsche the philologist was such a skilled crafter of words that even when translated from German to English, they pack quite a wallop. He was a master of the pithy aphorism.

Nietzsche asked startling questions and made bold pronouncements, but he did not question the limits of his own insight and wisdom nearly so much as of those he attacked. He threw around exotic ideas aplenty, but did not attend to their lack of logical coherence. Christianity was a religion for the weak, for lambs of slaughter, and for slaves, because it preaches restraint, self-denial, humility, and compassion.

Instead of Christ, Nietzsche presents the superman of the future who has the strength and power to take what he wants and enjoy what he takes. *And yet, none of us today are to be the superman.* Our role is merely to pave the path for him. Hence, Nietzsche preaches a self-sacrifice without a reward that we will ever see. The selfish egoist would have us become altruists, living our lives for somebody else, the superman of his egocentric dreams!

This was not for me, nor do many adolescent fans of Nietzsche remain died-in-the-wool adherents in adulthood, at least to my knowledge. Indeed, in the late 1970s and early '80s, when reading the philosophical side-musing of my muscular, mustachioed Mr. Universe mentor, Mike Mentzer, I could tell before he proclaimed it that he had moved beyond the imaginary more-than-human superman of Friedrich Nietzsche to the totally human (yet totally fictional) superheroes of another atheistic philosopher: Ayn Rand.

Still, it is not quite time for the interweaving of Ayn Rand's story with my own. A couple of other nonbelievers, a British philosopher and an American psychologist, must be considered first. So it's time to see if "the other Superman" wouldn't mind being a good sport and dash into a phone booth to fly us across the Atlantic to meet the Lord in the next chapter — Lord Bertrand Russell, that is.

TRUTH BOX #1

Apollo, Dionysus, and Truth

"Whatever a theologian feels to be true must *be false: this is almost a criterion of truth."*
FRIEDRICH NIETZSCHE, *The Antichrist*[15]

Nietzsche's first book, *The Birth of Tragedy* (1872), famously detailed two important philosophical tendencies or spirits we have inherited from the ancient Greeks. The Apollonian tendency, embodied in Apollo, the god of reason and light, stands for things like logic, order, control, symmetry, and quiet beauty of the sort embodied in sculpture. The Dionysian tendency, embodied in Dionysus, the god of wine, stands for things like excess, revelry, passion, and ecstatic joy of the sort embodied in singing and dancing. Many modern thinkers have made use of this contrast. Psychoanalyst Karen Horney used them to represent personality types. Psychologist William Smith even used them to represent orientations of different groups of weightlifters. Philosopher Ayn Rand (whom we'll consider in Chapter 4) used them to represent conflicting modern cultural values, using the superb and timely examples when she wrote comparing the scientific triumph of the aptly named Apollo 11 moon rocket to the Dionysian chaos that was the Woodstock music festival, both being events of 1969.

Nietzsche put himself into a very odd position as an arbiter of truth by siding with Dionysus over Apollo. He believed that Socrates and the rational, Apollonian philosophers who followed him represented a *degeneracy* in the Greek spirit that would crush the truths of passion when their ideas were taken to their logical conclusions in Christian theology.

Please stay tuned for Chapter 9, when we'll see how the greatest of theologians might reply to the self-styled "Antichrist's" claims of truth.

CHAPTER 2

The Lord and Lord Bertrand Russell

"My view is this: The good life is one inspired by love and guided by knowledge."

BERTRAND RUSSELL, *Why I Am Not a Christian*[1]

"Religious precepts date from a time when men were more cruel than they are and therefore tend to perpetuate inhumanities which the moral conscience of the age would otherwise outgrow."

BERTRAND RUSSELL, *Why I Am Not a Christian*[2]

"The books of Bertrand Russell are a modern substitute for the Bible."

TIME MAGAZINE[3]

I had signed up for "Issues on the Left" as a required Public Affairs Colloquia elective while pursuing my bachelor's degree in psychology. When it came to politics, I considered myself more "on the right," but the course fit well into my schedule and I thought it wouldn't hurt to hear what the other half thought. Early on in the course, when we had to describe two people, ideas, or symbols that had influenced us, I drew some looks of surprise (and a few of disgust) from my Marxist-leaning classmates when I first mentioned the American flag. How could I be inspired by such a thing? These were the early Reagan years, mind you, and American business and enterprise were again thriving, which many there interpreted as just so much more oppression of the masses. I simply said that because of the principles this flag represents and the people who have defended it, we are able to have a class like this criticizing our institutions, and that courses like it are not likely taking place in countries way to the left, behind the still-standing metaphorical Iron Curtain and the literal, physical Berlin Wall.

Anyway, I was redeemed to some extent when I named my second influence, that of the British mathematician turned philosopher and social reformer, Lord Bertrand Russell. Indeed, our professor revealed that Russell was one of his own great formative influences.

Why Russell? For one thing, I was captivated by the first quotation that starts this chapter. The fundamentals for a good life, according to Russell, were knowledge and love — this being a very noble sentiment, and quite inspirational to one of a sensitive and intellectual temperament.

Bertrand Russell (1872-1970) was born to atheistic, free-thinking parents, Lord John Russell and Lady Katherine Amberley. His father died of bronchitis, following a prolonged bout of depression, when Bertrand was only 2 years old, and his mother died of diphtheria when he was only 3. Both parents were quite "progressive" in their views. They championed birth control, for example, and his mother carried on an affair with the children's tutor — purportedly with their father's approval. They insisted on burials with no Christian rites and willed that Bertrand and an older brother be raised by like-minded guardians after their deaths. A court decided, however, that the Russell children would be raised by his elderly grandfather, who died two years later, and by his Scotch Presbyterian, later Unitarian, grandmother.

Russell had written extensively about his early years in his autobiography. I've dipped back into some of his brief biographical essays, but have not returned to the multivolume, complete autobiography itself. I'll discuss very soon some of the ideas that appealed to me, but I cannot forget at this point a few things that struck me as unappealing, even as I read them in my own late teen, freethinking years.

First, Russell painted a very gloomy view of his lonely childhood and adolescence, noting repeated bouts of suicidal thoughts, and he reported on his own sexual behaviors with little sense of dignity or shame. Further, though it would be years before I would have a wife of my own, I was struck with revulsion by an incident that this prophet of enlightened love for humanity described regarding his own first wife. He reported that he was out for a bicycle ride one day and decided matter-of-factly that he no longer loved her, and he told her so, though they remained married for several more years. It made me wonder even then, what did this Nobel Prize-winning genius for literature think love really meant? Isn't love more something *we do and will* than something that just does (or doesn't) *happen to us*?

Love and Knowledge

Russell is probably most famous for his attacks on religion and traditional morality, championing modern methods of philosophy and science as the means of liberating us from what he saw as the primitive, superstitious, and cruel doctrines of traditional religion in general, and Christianity in particular. Among his most famous works is the collection of essays entitled *Why I Am Not a Christian*.

When I recently started rereading this book, I was more than a little dismayed, wondering how I had ever considered these ideas profound. Of course, I read them the first time through adolescent glasses that had but briefly glanced at the history of theology and Christianity, and now my spectacles have seen so much more. Russell, of course, though a brilliant man, was in his 50s when he penned many of those words. It appears to me now that Christianity remained his greatest blind spot. Still, as early as 1925, in the essay "What I Believe," Russell had penned the inspiring line cited at the start of this chapter: "The good life is one inspired by love and guided by knowledge." What, then, did he mean?

Lord Russell starts by explaining that either love or knowledge alone just will not do. His example of *knowledge without love* is simply "the late war," World War I. His example of *love without knowledge* is the purported medieval practice that when a pestilence spread throughout a land, holy men would urge the populace to gather into churches to pray, thus spreading the pestilence.

(This was quite characteristic of Russell, by the way. Almost without fail, he would pull from the history of Christianity only the most unusual and negative examples, whether factual or not. His writings are rife with these slams — and even his own daughter, Katherine Tait, who later became a Christian and wrote a memoir of her father, reported that he would discuss only what he saw as Christianity's greatest errors, and would never address the most profound of its greatest messages. Many of these "errors," it turns out, reveal Russell's own credulity or lack of knowledge of the subject matter.)

Russell continues that while love and knowledge are necessary, love is, in a sense, more fundamental, because it will motivate people to seek knowledge to find out how to help those they love. He goes on to describe two key characteristics of love as "*delight*" and "*well-wishing*." We experience delight in the contemplation of things we love, and we have feelings of intense benevolence toward those whom we love. Russell gives extreme examples of men who have sacrificed themselves to help lepers, as well as the everyday example of parental love. Hence, love is a strong desire for another person's welfare.

Now, these are wonderful and noble feelings, and in his writings Russell contrasts them with what he portrays as the hurtful and superstitious ethical principles of Christianity. Just last night I reread Russell's chapter on St. Thomas Aquinas from Russell's *History of Western Philosophy*. In his summary of St. Thomas's massive *Summa Theologica*, Lord Russell did *not* mention the fact that St. Thomas wrote about 500 pages on the subject of *virtues*. St. Thomas made a monumental, rigorously reasoned contribution to the classical philosophical tradition of virtue ethics, and Lord Russell chose to completely ignore it. Here, we'll avoid that egregious omission!

Writing 700 years before Russell, and basing his ideas on those of Aristotle and Scripture composed more than a millennia earlier, St. Thomas describes three classes of virtue: intellectual, moral, and theological.

The chief intellectual virtue is *wisdom*. Its object, or goal, is truth, and it stands on the twin pillars of the virtues of knowledge and understanding.

The chief moral virtue is *prudence*. Its object, or goal, is the good, and it is the practical wisdom that enables us to choose and employ the right means to obtain worthy ends.

The chief theological (God-given) virtue is *charity*, and it is the most fundamental of all the virtues. It sets the goals for all, and "the principal act of charity is to love."[4]

Further, in describing charity, St. Thomas expounds in great detail about the element that Russell calls "delight," explaining, for example, just how "joy" is an "effect" of charity, and how contemplation of God, the highest possible object of love, brings about the highest possible happiness. St. Thomas also knows well the "benevolence," or well-wishing, component of love — and then some. In fact, one of my favorite quotations from St. Thomas reads: "Now the love of our neighbor requires that not only should we be our neighbor's well-wishers, but also his well-doers."[5]

We can see, then, that Russell's view on love and knowledge is, in fact, though wise, far from anything new, and immeasurably far from being opposed to the core beliefs of Christianity. But another of those moral virtues that St. Thomas writes about is the virtue of justice, justice being defined as "giving each one his rightful due."[6] Did Russell deal justly with Christianity in his writings? I don't think so. Let's consider a few examples.

With Liberty and Justice for All?

Bertrand Russell's philosophy was much about liberty and freedom. He saw himself as helping people free themselves from the shackles of religious oppression, opening up the way to liberation, and to freedom of thought and behavior in a variety of areas, including, among the most important, that of sexuality. His views on sexuality are rather self-contradictory, and varied greatly over the years. He often prided himself on his ability to change his mind, though I wonder if he thought much about the damage he might have caused others by boldly proclaiming harmful views that he later discarded.

Russell denigrated the idea of celibacy, that one would forgo sexual behavior for a higher ideal, yet he argued against sex without love, on the purely animal level, arguing that it could not bring satisfaction. He conducted many extramarital affairs and did not condemn adultery, yet he reported distress when one of his wives had been adulterous.

Without unjustly implying that this characterizes the level of *all* of Russell's pronouncements, I think it is only fair to offer a few examples of Russell's own practical recommendations for implementing knowledge and love — though he did not have the excuse of living in the proverbial dark and superstitious Middle Ages.

Let's consider, for example, his recommendations for curbing a modern pestilence, that of venereal diseases. Many decades ago, Russell wrote in "The Place of Sex Among Human Values" that besides reducing legal prostitution and promoting advances in medicine, curbing venereal disease "can best be effected by that greater freedom among young people which has been growing up in recent years."[7]

I think we can agree that professional prostitution remains relatively rare, medicine has certainly advanced, and so has sexual freedom among the young. Venereal disease rates, unfortunately, have skyrocketed, rather than declined. Further, with the concomitant rise in divorce rates and instances of children raised without both parents — and despite the widespread availability and use of contraception — have come unprecedented rates of abortion. It seems that Russell, too, has unwittingly encouraged more than one plague of his own.

On Human Nature (And Its Non-Existence)

Many atheists deny not only *God*, but in a sense *man* as well. In addition, while many atheists castigate religious believers for their credulity and naiveté, they sometimes toss around some real whoppers of their own. I refer to the second quotation at the beginning of this chapter as an example of both. Russell declared that religion was a relic of bygone times, when man was less mature, and much more cruel, than he was at the time — namely, 1927. Unfortunately, this was penned not long before the nightmare worlds of atheistic Nazi and communist regimes exterminated more innocent human lives in a few decades than had all of the world's religions since the beginning of recorded history. Woe to the victims of the enlightened moral conscience of that age.

Russell certainly did not approve of such atrocities, but we can be sure that ideas falsely portraying the nature of Christianity, and the nature of man, were fuel for their fires. Russell was awarded the 1950 Nobel Prize in Literature for his various "humanitarian" writings. I think he genuinely intended to do good — and some good he did do. I'll address some of that in the next section. For now, though, I'd like to point out a contradiction: this great humanitarian, who sought nothing more than to spread the love of man, also had a rather lowly opinion of said object of love — man himself, that is. For example, in arguing against those who see purpose in the process of evolution, and who point to a higher and more glorious being in man, he cites examples of man — including Hitler, Caligula, and Nero — and refers to man as "this lame and impotent conclusion."[8]

I guess there is a certain kind of equal fairness (or unfairness), as Russell portrays both Christianity and man by the worst examples. Russell, too, as we can see, was no fan of the superman. He considered how small man was compared to the stars, but was not sufficiently impressed with (or thankful for) our unique powers to perceive, understand, and contemplate those shining heavenly bodies.

But what of "human nature?" Well, along with many progressive-minded atheists, Russell argues that there really is no fixed "human nature." He argues that differences in customs and habits, and in rules of right and wrong, among members of different cultures provide evidence for this — but this position neglects the observation that all cultures have some form of moral code of right and wrong, and that most are quite in line with many of the Ten Commandments. He also argues that we are not fundamentally different from the lower animals, that free will is an illusion, and that all of our behaviors are determined ultimately by prior events outside of us. To improve the human condition, then, all we need to do is improve the social and material conditions of our environment. And in case you're wondering if I'm exaggerating his position, note that in regards to fear and hatred — which Russell believed were promulgated by the Church — he declared that "these emotions can now be almost wholly eliminated from human nature by educational, economic, and political reforms."[9]

Well, we've seen how the great atheistic humanitarian projects of the 20th century turned out. It seems that external circumstances have not yet been so configured as to completely elevate our consciences and tame our fears and hatreds. We'll return to the issues of human nature and free will when we examine the writings of biologist Richard Dawkins — and those of the Stoics and St. Thomas Aquinas as well.

The Wisdom Literature of the Bible: Lord Russell Version

I'm just playing here on *Time* magazine's decades-old description of Russell's books as modern substitutes for the Bible. When Lord Russell was not making snide witticisms at a straw man Christianity's expense, he could indeed engage in entertaining and practically useful philosophizing. A book that I admired — and still do, in regards to many passages — is his practical, commonsense guide: *The Conquest of Happiness*. And in one passage, he actually praises the Bible!

Russell believed that one thing which leads to modern man's unhappiness is his perceived need for perpetual stimulation and excitement, with a concurrent incapacity to tolerate boredom — indeed, "a generation that cannot endure boredom will be a generation of little men."[10] He argues that having a noble purpose should enable us to endure long periods of effort, struggle, and sometimes, boredom. Every great book, for example, has its relatively boring passages. Here is where his surprising tribute to the Bible comes in. He reports an imaginary publisher receiving the manuscript of the Old Testament for the first time. The publisher is impressed with the beginning, but then, fearing the reader's boredom at things like genealogies, he advises the author to "pick out the highlights, take out the superfluous matter, and bring me back your manuscript when you have reduced it to a reasonable length."[11]

Here is another surprising snippet from a promoter of experimental sexuality: "Love is an experience in which our whole being is renewed and refreshed as is that of plants by rain after drought.... Love is part of the life of Earth; sex without love is not."[12] And these are surprising lines from one of the early advocates of birth control: "They do not, on the average, have so much as two children per marriage; they do not enjoy life enough to wish to beget children.... Those whose outlook on life causes them to feel so little happiness that they do not care to beget children are biologically doomed. Before very long they must be succeeded by something gayer and jollier."[13]

In his chapter on fatigue, Russell, though a denier of free will, also made some very useful comments on human psychology, focusing on our ability to control our own thoughts and emotions. Indeed, these ideas would profoundly influence psychologist Albert Ellis — our focus of the next chapter — and these ideas themselves were influenced by the much earlier writings of the Stoics we'll meet five chapters down this road.

Russell was a critic of the concept of sin. Christians believe that sin, which leads us away from God, produces unhappiness. Russell, believing there is no God, argued that it is not sinful behavior, but rather *the sense of sin*, the very notion that it is possible to behave in a way that is contrary to God's will, that leads to man's unhappiness. Ironically, though, while Russell would have us throw the very idea of sin out the window, he included in his book on happiness a chapter on the avoidance of envy.

Envy, you see, is one of the seven "capital," or deadly, sins the great Church Fathers have warned about for millennia. Indeed, it seems that Russell and the Church are on the same page when it comes to the fact that envy is deadly to our happiness.

Regarding the envious man, Russell states that "instead of deriving pleasure from what he has, he derives pain from what others have."[14] He rightly notes that the envious tend to think too much in terms of comparison with others, and that cures include a sense of admiration for the greatness of others and a diminished focus on one's self.

Russell's prescriptions for happiness include finding a zestful sense of joyful interest in people and things outside of one's self, developing the capacity for some form of skilled work, and developing a sense of affection for one's fellow man. He writes that "for my own part, speaking personally, I have found the happiness of parenthood greater than any other that I have experienced."[15]

I think that what has come to disappoint and dismay me upon my return to the writings of Bertrand Russell is to see that he perceived the best, most useful, and most humane of his ideas as somehow conflicting with the message of Christ. I disagree with his sense of fundamental disagreement with Christianity, and that is why I am not a Russellian any more.

Digging into Bertrand Russell's writings after all these years was a bit like coming across a vein of kryptonite. There is an element there of weakness, despair, and belittlement of God and of man, and it is born of this lover of knowledge's lack of love for and knowledge about the Christianity he disparaged. Ironically, it was one of Russell's followers, American psychologist Albert Ellis, who helped make me stronger and render me less vulnerable to all of life's assaults, when I struck upon his writings in my early 20s. Let's move up and away to him next.

TRUTH BOX #2

Answering Russell's Question

"Has Religion Made Useful Contributions to Civilization?"[16]

This was the title of one of Bertrand Russell's essays, first published in 1930. Russell's answer in a nutshell was "No!" — and I *almost* believed him! Of course, I almost believed him because, sadly, though educated in the Catholic school system, I knew surprisingly little about Church history and heritage. If you'd like to dig into some very detailed answers, I'll refer you to Thomas E. Wood's *How the Catholic Church Built Western Civilization* and to H. W. Crocker III's *Triumph: The Power and the Glory of the Catholic Church*. Off the top of my head, though, I'll offer a few examples. One is the establishment of hospitals and charities for the sick and the poor. Indeed, in the fourth century, *after* Emperor Constantine the Great had legalized Christianity within the Roman Empire, a subsequent emperor, Julian, a former Arian Christian turned Cynic philosopher and follower of the cult of Mithras, when attempting to overthrow Christianity and reinstate the ancient gods, had no choice but to advise his followers to imitate the "Galileans" in their charitable and hospitable establishments. (You can read about it in Julian's ancient anti-Christian book, *Against the Galileans*.)

Other examples of the Church's contributions to Western civilization include:

- The preservation of the written wisdom of the ancient Greek and Roman worlds through the works of Catholic scribe monks.

- The establishment of the European university system in the Middle Ages.
- The re-introduction of the thought of Aristotle by the Scholastic philosophers.
- The preservation and adaptation of the ancient art of memorization techniques by St. Albert the Great and St. Thomas Aquinas.
- Multiple contributions to astronomy by Jesuit priests.
- The discovery of the basic principles of genetics by Benedictine monk Gregor Mendel.

Please excuse me, but I've run out of time here!

CHAPTER 3

Albert Ellis: Reason, Emotion, Psychotherapy, and Jehovah

"Although we can have no certainty *that God does or does not exist, we have an exceptionally high degree of probability that He or She doesn't. This is exactly the same degree we have in thinking that there* most probably *is no Santa Claus, no fairies, no angels, and no devil. There could be — but it is most improbable."*

ALBERT ELLIS, *Rational Emotive Behavior Therapy: It Works for Me — It Can Work for You*[1]

"Oh yes, I'm very happy. I like my work and I like various aspects of it — going around the world, teaching the gospel according to St. Albert. I like that. And seeing clients, doing group therapy, writing books."

ALBERT ELLIS, *Rational Emotive Behavior Therapy: It Works for Me — It Can Work for You*[2]

The television Superman I grew up with was a class act all the way. For one thing, I don't recall him ever getting particularly angry when criminals did things like fire at him point blank with their pistols. No, there he stood, fists on hips, chest stuck out, with a slightly bemused expression and perhaps a slight shake of the head, as one might do when telling a naughty child, "Tsk-tsk, you know you shouldn't do that," while he calmly relieved them of their weapons. What an ideal for young boys — to become invincible, not only in body, but in spirit. Not only were those criminals unable to do him bodily harm, but they couldn't even ruffle his composure!

Of course, no child is made of steel, and rarely must he grapple with dangerous criminals on any kind of regular basis. Still, we all face threats and fears and challenges of various sorts, in one way or another, every day of our lives. And what we tend to fear most is not only bodily harm, but also emotional trauma from other people's actions toward us, and their reactions to our own perceived shortcomings, quirks, or failures. As a child, we might ask: "What if he tries to bully me again when we get off the bus?" "What if I fail that test at school?" "What if I strike out again in Little League?" "What if the kids laugh at that new outfit Mom made me wear?" A little later we might ask: "What if she turns me down when I ask her out?" "What if I get a poor job-performance evaluation?" Or maybe "What if people laugh or are bored to tears when I have to give that presentation?"

We all have fears of some sort or other. One of the most common is the last that I mentioned: the fear of public speaking. If you couple this common fear of being placed in a position of public scrutiny with an especially emotionally sensitive individual temperament, you have the formula for some major stage fright.

I was that way myself in my teens and early 20s. I would rather have climbed a mountain of kryptonite than give a talk in public. In fact, though certainly wishing them no harm, even in my first years of college, when I had a speech to give at the end of the semester, I'd consider the odds that the professor might become ill, and that the speech assignment would fall by the wayside. I barely spoke in class in high school, prompting my algebra teacher to call me "the silent genius" (not as bad, I suppose, as the "dumb ox" label St. Thomas Aquinas had been given by his schoolmates). Anyway, coming from a family with a strong streak of shyness about such things (to which some might today apply the fancy clinical label of "social phobia"), I remember cousins being shocked when they heard that I had started teaching college classes, and later doing radio and television spots.

What brought about the change in me? It was in my early 20s, while studying the psychological theories of a slight, elderly, diabetic man — who, ironically, emphasized human fallibility and frailty — that I learned how to let the fears of public speaking and many other things bounce off my most un-steely chest.

Albert Ellis Bids Freud *Auf Wiedersehen*

Albert Ellis (1913-2007), a clinical psychologist, was a practicing psychoanalyst in the 1940s. The "scientific" theories of Sigmund Freud's psychoanalysis were the fad of the day in psychiatry and clinical psychology, and Ellis had been formally trained in the classical methods. His clients would lie upon his couch, as he, being as passive and nondirective as possible, would subtly encourage them to relate their childhood stories, their free-flowing thoughts, and the stories of their dreams. He noted that sometimes clients would eventually reach a kind of "Aha!" moment — with one man coming to believe, for example, that the real reason he had not been motivated to work as an adult was actually due to an unrealized, but deep-seated and long-held hatred of his father from early childhood. "Aha! Eureka! *That* is why!" The only problem was that once the man achieved this insight, he still did not get out and go to work!

Though relatively successful as a psychoanalyst, helping some clients improve their lives through bringing unconscious motivations up to the level of their conscious awareness, Ellis was dissatisfied with his own success rate. He felt at times that rather than sitting back silently with pen in hand, he should be sitting face-to-face with his clients and discussing things and actively advising them. He eventually went on to build a system of psychotherapy that did just such things, working much more quickly and effectively than psychoanalysis. Interestingly, his method owed the most to the philosophy of the Stoics, which we will address in Chapter 7 — and perhaps even more interesting, it grew out of his own recollections of how he had trained himself in his youth to work up the courage to speak to young women!

So what was the secret to diminishing one's fears and all sorts of emotional disturbances? Let's take to the streets of your own hometown to find out.

There she is! She's walking down the sidewalk on the other side of the street. She's looking your way, and you smile and begin to wave. But alas, there she goes. Not a smile, not a wave, just plain *nada*! There you are, perhaps a bit embarrassed (*Did other people see that snub?*), or saddened (*I guess I don't rate with her*), or maybe a little angry (*How could she slight me like that?*). Now let's look at this little incident psychologically, and alphabetically.

At the same time that Freud reigned over American psychiatry, behaviorists reigned over psychology. These were the folks who built on the foundation of Russian Ivan Pavlov's experiments with salivating dogs, to explain human behaviors in terms of *stimulus-response* (S-R) pairings. Give Fido some tasty food, or even something like a bell that he associates with food (*stimulus*), and out comes the salivatory behavior (*response*). Applying this scenario to our example, Sally does not acknowledge you or me (*stimulus*), and so we're embarrassed, or sad, or angry, or perhaps all three (*response*).

Of course, some perceptive psychologists argued from the start that we're not really just stimulus-response (S-R) machines. Something does in fact happen inside us between the "S" and the "R." This leads to S-O-R models, where "O" is the organism itself. When you and I respond to Sally's slight, something goes on inside us — and what is that? Well, consider things like those questions and comments I posed: "Did other people see that snub?" "I guess I don't rate with her." "How could she slight me like that?" These thoughts, beliefs, or self-statements reflect the processes of the "O" that come between the "S" and the "R," and these are what ultimately determine what our response will be, both in how we feel and how we act.

When We Know Our ABCs, It Won't Matter Quite So Much *What You Think of Me!*

What Ellis did was to boil these scenarios down to their simple ABCs. Here's how.

Let "S" (the stimulus) be "A" (an *Activating event*), and let "R" (the response) be "C" (the emotional/behavioral *Consequence*). When Sally passes by (A) and we are embarrassed or sad or angry (C), we tend to act as if "A" caused "C" — but Ellis points out the often-neglected, but most important true causal factor. Let the activities of the organism (O) be represented here by "B" (our *Beliefs*). Sally did not cause us to feel a certain way. We actually did it to ourselves!

How can we show this? Let's say, for example, that while you walk on all disgruntled, you soon see Sally getting out of her car on your side of the street, and she beams you a smile and calls you over. Oops! That wasn't Sally after all. Are you still sad or mad at her? Or let's say it was Sally. You see her later and she tells you that she just got back from the eye doctor and her eyes were dilated, or she wasn't wearing her contacts, or she just heard some tragic news and was lost in thought. Are you still sad or mad?

This is one simple way we can see how our beliefs determine our emotional reactions.

Let's Not Step on Any Toes

Another very simple and vivid example Ellis used is this one. Let's say a huge man steps on your foot as he passes you in a crowded bus (A) without a word of apology. Might you be angry (C)? But what if you then noticed his dark glasses and white cane? Would your belief (B) change and your anger diminish with it?

All right. But Ellis's system of psychotherapy goes much deeper than this. He does not just advise us to make sure that our beliefs (B's) accurately reflect activating events (A's). What if Sally really did snub us? What if that big dude was not blind and actually enjoys crunching people's toes? Must we still become embarrassed, or sad, or angry? More accurately stated, must we still *make ourselves* embarrassed, or sad, or angry? Ellis answers with an emphatic no!

If we became embarrassed, sad, or angry only when we suffered true injustices of various sorts, well, as fallible as we all are, we would still go around embarrassed, sad, or angry a good deal of the time! Further, Ellis notes that when we suffer various slights or ills, insults or injuries, we tend to ruminate and keep thinking about the incidents, stacking one irrational belief upon the other as we talk to ourselves about it. If we feel slighted, we might start questioning our own worth: *Hmmm, didn't so-and-so also slight me last week?* If we feel angry, we might start cataloging Sally's other faults and work ourselves up against her. We might even realize at some point that we are being a bit unreasonable, but then start to bash ourselves for it: *Oh, I always overreact! What a sad specimen I am!*

Ellis states that many irrational and self-harming beliefs are common to humanity. When upset, for example, we tend to "awfulize." We make situations out to be worse than they really are. Let's take the public speaking example. We might think it would be "awful' or "horrible" if we did poorly. Ellis would advise that we give it our best shot and realize that it would only be "mildly unfortunate" and not "awful" if we failed.

Here are a couple of ways you could actually apply this. Let's say you have to give a speech. Relax, and imagine this scene if you will: You stand in the crowded room, mumble and mispronounce your first words, crack a joke that meets with silence, knock over your glass of water, realize that you've accidentally spit a bit on the folks in the first row, and when you look down you realize you have put on two different shoes that don't match — and your zipper is down. Try to vividly imagine this scenario and also imagine yourself saying something like this: *Oh well, nobody's perfect! That would not be fun, but it wouldn't be awful either. I would not be the world's greatest public speaker. I might even be the worst, but somebody's gotta be, I suppose, and life would still go on.*

If we can train ourselves to accept even imagined worst-case scenarios, we can train ourselves to handle the lesser problems that may well arise.

This is what I did myself, by the way. Being of a rather high-strung, sensitive, and nervous temperament by birth, when speaking in public my body would rebel against me by making my face flush, my voice falter, and my heart pound within my chest. Of course, I would fear that people would notice these things (which, of course, they did). The last presentation that I faced with such fear, trepidation, and bodily rebellion was during my junior year in college. When I got up, I simply asked the class to bear with me if they could see my heart pounding within my chest, and I got on with it. From that day on, I would get the occasional flutter (which even Cicero, the greatest of Roman orators, reported he would feel before a speech), but it has never been a big deal for me. And I've never felt "awful" about the prospect of a speech again! I had actually chosen to make the supposedly "horrible" consequence happen — that people would realize I was really nervous — and in doing so, I realized that it really was no big deal. Ever since that experience, I have focused on my subject matter, not on myself!

Another irrational-thinking tendency Ellis points out is our tendency to become *demanding* of others, blaming other people for our own emotional distress and self-harming behaviors: "You made me angry!" We also make demands on ourselves: "I must not get nervous before I ask a girl out!" Here, Ellis says we act as if we were "Jehovah," setting up the laws of the universe for others and ourselves. Mind you, Scripture scholars indicate that the very term "Jehovah" is a corrupted and inaccurate word used to translate an ancient name for God. Whether or not Ellis knew this, he preferred to use this term to represent his own corrupted and inaccurate understanding of God as some kind of a bully in the sky.

Anyway, Ellis notes that there are many ways that we can train our minds to catch ourselves when we are upsetting ourselves through our self-statements based on irrational, self-defeating beliefs. One way is a very careful use of language. Don't tell yourself it would be "awful" if you failed, but that it would be "unfortunate." Don't say "She must do what I want!" but instead "It would be nice if she would go along with me in this matter, and unpleasant if she didn't, but life will go on!"

He also recommends the avoidance of rating one's self-worth and putting oneself down for one's failings. He says we should not focus on "*self*-esteem," because our focus should be outward, on tasks, rather than inward, on our own egos. In essence, Ellis urges us to question or dispute (there's the "D" in the model) our irrational beliefs, replacing them with sane, healthy, rational beliefs that will lead to healthier emotional consequences and behaviors — and I believe he is jolly well right!

Let's lay it out in alphabetical order.

The ABCs of Emotional Disturbance (And Healing)				
A	B	C	D	E
ACTIVATING EVENT	BELIEFS (IRRATIONAL)	EMOTIONAL CONSE- QUENCE	DISPUTATION OF BELIEFS	NEW EMOTIONAL CONSE- QUENCE
Sally actually snubs me	I don't rate. How terrible!	Sad	That's her opinion! So what?	Mild disap- pointment
	How dare she! How wicked!	Angry	That's her problem! I'll pray for her.	Concern for Sally
Blind guy steps on foot.	The careless oaf should watch his step!	Angry	It was an ac- cident. How courageous of him to travel alone.	Forgiveness and admira- tion

Ellis's Irrational Beliefs *About Christianity*

There is a great deal that is good and helpful in Albert Ellis's Rational Emotive Behavior Therapy (REBT), and I'll highlight additional similar ideas when we come to the Stoics. But now it is time to come to the place where I part ways with Ellis's philosophy, if not his psychology.

Ellis was raised in a non-practicing Jewish household. He wrote that he was highly influenced by philosopher Bertrand Russell, whom we met in the last chapter. He felt that religion in general — and Christianity in particular — encouraged and systematized the kinds of irrational beliefs we use to disturb ourselves. Quoting with approval from a 1956 sociology text entitled *Problems in American Society*, Ellis wrote the following:

[M]any of our most cherished and dogmatically upheld values — such as monogamous marriage, freedom, acquisitiveness, democracy, education, monotheistic religion, technology and science — are only assumed to be "good" values and are rarely seriously reviewed or questioned by those who keep drumming them into the heads of our children.[3]

History, of course, has shown that such values would soon be questioned aplenty, but with an associated *skyrocketing increase* of "problems in American society," including divorce, abortion, incarceration, and burgeoning government encroachment on new areas of life.

Further, Ellis argued that the belief in God was an irrational and "dubious hypothesis," noting that

millions of people, for example, believe wholeheartedly and dogmatically in the existence of God when, as Hume, Kant, Russell and many other first-rate philosophers have shown, they can't possibly ever prove his existence. But that hardly ever stops them from fervently believing.[4]

Now, I bought into this line of thinking in the 1980s. You see, I was unaware of other quite substantial, "first-rate" philosophers who did not consider the hypothesis of God's existence quite so "dubious" or improvable. Let's jump ahead 23 years to agnostic social scientist Charles Murray's 2003 survey entitled *Human Accomplishment: The Pursuit of Excellence in the Arts and Sciences, 800 B.C. to 1950.*[5]

Murray tracked references to great thinkers and achievers in multiple fields of art and science over a time span of more than two millennia, and he then systematically and objectively placed individuals in rank order according to their influence in fields as diverse as astronomy, biology, chemistry, physics, mathematics, Indian philosophy, and Chinese art, just to name a few. It's pretty intriguing stuff. We find that in the realm of philosophy, Aristotle and Plato, two believers in God, are rated number one and number two, respectively, of all philosophers, ranking above Kant. St. Thomas Aquinas, the patron saint of scholars, is rated higher than Hume. And other theists, including St. Augustine and Socrates, rank far above Bertrand Russell. So, if Ellis himself was going to argue from authority, perhaps he should have chosen some more authoritative authorities!

Next, let's take a quick look at a few of what Ellis described as 11 extremely common irrational ideas that people in our culture typically say to themselves to keep themselves disturbed. These are but a sample, mind you. Ellis noted that he once came up with a list of 259 common irrational ideas!

In the table that follows, I'm going to give you Ellis's first five irrational beliefs in the left column — and by the way, I think he is completely correct about these five being common and disturbing irrational ideas. I still believe that it is helpful if we can detect and combat these ideas in our own thinking. This is useful, practical stuff, even for Christians.

That is where the second column on "Scriptural Advice" comes in. *What I'm disputing is not the prevalence and importance of these irrational beliefs in causing psychological disturbance, but rather Ellis's assumptions that these beliefs are fostered and endorsed by Christian teaching.* Here, I have merely selected one or two sample quotations from dozens or hundreds of possibilities, to show that others had argued against these irrational beliefs long before he did, these others being not only the Greek and Roman Stoics, but also the authors of the divinely inspired Scriptures. So, let's look at the first five of the eleven irrational commandments we give to ourselves, and then see what happens when irrationality meets reason *and faith.*

Is Christianity Irrational?	
IRRATIONAL BELIEFS[6]	SCRIPTURAL ADVICE
Irrational Belief #1: *"It is a dire necessity for adult humans to be loved or approved by virtually every significant other person in their community."*	"Blessed are you when men revile you and persecute you and utter all kinds of evil against you falsely on my account." (Mt 5:11)
Irrational Belief #2: *"One absolutely must be competent, adequate, and achieving in all important respects or else one is an inadequate, worthless person."*	"Whoever humbles himself like this child, he is the greatest in the kingdom of heaven." (Mt 18:4)
Irrational Belief #3: *"People absolutely must act considerately and fairly, and they are damnable villains if they do not. They are their bad acts."*	"Let him who is without sin among you be the first to throw a stone at her." (Jn 8:7)
Irrational Belief #4: *"It is awful and terrible when things are not the way one would very much like them to be."*	Instead you ought to say, "If the Lord wills, we shall live and we shall do this or that." (Jas 4:15)
Irrational Belief #5: *"Emotional disturbance is mainly externally caused, and people have little or no ability to increase or decrease their dysfunctional feelings and behaviors."*	And if any one loves righteousness, her labors are virtues; for she teaches self-control and prudence, justice and courage; nothing in life is more profitable for men than these. (Wis 8:7)

As for Irrational Belief #1, if we tell ourselves that everyone must love us, we haven't picked that up from the Scriptures or the Church. Jesus told us that those who follow Him may well face persecution, rather than love, from their neighbors. We are commanded *to love* our neighbor, with no guarantees that our neighbor will love us in return. Christ's Church was built by martyrs, and his own death was the first.

Irrational Belief #2, though no doubt prevalent in the minds of modern men, is contradicted by a multitude of Scriptures instilling in us the virtue of humility. Those who place themselves first will be last. We are to seat ourselves at the seat of least honor. We don't love little children because of their great accomplishments. We love their innate goodness, wonder, and faith in us. We do not have to prove our worth to God.

Regarding Irrational Belief #3, Scripture tells us to condemn the sin, but not the sinner, since none of us are in a position to cast any stones. Jesus forgave the adulteress herself, but He did tell her to go and sin no more. Jesus also praised the woman with a sinful history over the proud Pharisee when she anointed the Lord with oil and washed His feet with her tears (Lk 7:36-50). God does not tell us to vilify and hate people. The Church has for centuries considered it a spiritual work of mercy to advise and, if necessary, reprove one another for sinful behaviors — but we are not to judge our neighbor as a person, lest we be judged. Thus, the third irrational idea is not endorsed in the teachings of Christ.

Nor are Christians advised to hold Irrational Belief #4 and exhibit low frustration tolerance when things don't go their way. The idea of accepting God's will, expressed in the Letter of James and elsewhere, was presented by 20th-century martyr St. Maximilian Kolbe as a simple formula: $v = V$ (with *voluntas* being Latin for "will"), where the small "v" stands for your will and the large "V" for God's will. The Christian saint will strive to live by that formula, and every Christian is called to be a saint. This was the key to the exceedingly high tolerance for unpleasant events that enabled Father Kolbe to volunteer to replace a family man randomly selected to be starved to death in a Nazi concentration camp.

As for Irrational Belief #5, the Christian is not taught to blame others for his emotional disturbances. Rather, he is taught to build and hone the powers and capacities within himself to control his own emotions and behaviors — building within himself the perfection of will, called *justice*, that seeks to give all their rightful due; the mastering of the concupiscible, or desiring, appetite, called *temperance*, that enables us to control our desires for things like food and sex; the mastering of the irascible, or aggressive, appetite, called *fortitude*, that enables us to muster up the courage to do difficult deeds to serve the good; and the perfection of practical reason, called *prudence*, that allows us to wisely choose the right means to serve good ends. The wise man of the Old and the New Testaments is a man who has "died to self" and learned to bring his feelings and behaviors under control.

Ellis also urges us to avoid an obsessive "perfectionism" — and in this, Christians can also agree. We are called to be "perfect" by Jesus himself, but this does not mean we can be completely infallible, flawless, and sinless. It means that we are to be open to God's grace, to help us become as "perfect" (deriving from the Latin verb *perficere* — to make complete) as we can be within the limits of our human nature. We are called to make ourselves complete by perfecting our God-given powers through the virtues. Since virtues, by definition, perfect our abilities to bring our actions under the rule of right reason, no virtue is opposed to reason — that is, no virtue is irrational.

Ellis described himself as an atheist, rather than an agnostic, since he believed that the probability of God's existence was very low — "something like .000000001 percent."[7] (He didn't reveal how he did the math.) He long held that religious belief itself is irrational and of necessity leads to mental disturbance. Over time, though, he admitted, in the face of mounting evidence, that religious beliefs "*sometimes* help people mentally and emotionally,"[8] and he even co-authored a book on using Rational Emotive Behavior Therapy with religious clients, relating that he was actually opposed to "fanaticism" in religion "and in almost anything,"[9] rather than religion per se.

I believe that elements of Ellis's Rational Emotive Behavior Therapy can be effectively employed by Catholics, but I also maintain its most profound lessons were borrowed from the ancient Stoic philosophers who devoutly sought to follow God's will. We'll check them out a few chapters from now. Next, however, we'll check out another avowed atheist who apparently raised the ire of Albert Ellis himself. I had read Ellis's 1968 book on her philosophy, *Is Objectivism a Religion?* I learned a few years back, though, that while Ellis had toned down his anti-religious rhetoric somewhat, his vilification of our next philosopher had apparently grown, at least if we judge by the title of his re-write of the *Objectivism* book, complete with its less-than-fully-complimentary new title: *Ayn Rand: Her Fascistic and Fanatically Religious Philosophy.* Up, up, and away we'll go again then, this time to meet the so-called fascist, fanatic philosopher herself. (I'll let you decide!)

TRUTH BOX #3

Are the Odds Against God?

The probability of God's existence is very low, "something like .000000001 percent."[10]

Albert Ellis often chided his neurotic clients for acting like "Jehovah." Jehovah, for Ellis, represented irrational extremes of "demandingness," expecting others, one's self, and the universe to behave exactly how one demands — and pronto! As we see above, Ellis also thought that the odds that there actually was an all-powerful God were very, very small, though he never does say exactly how he derived his eight zeroes, meaning one in a billion. The arbitrary "one in a billion" estimate is also favored by scientist Richard Dawkins for various sorts of things, such as the likelihood that there is life on a given planet — we know, of course, that there is life on this one!

Another thing that both Ellis and Dawkins hold in common is their concept of a big mean bully, Jehovah, who most likely does not exist. Fair enough, but I wonder how deeply they had studied the name from which some say Jehovah was a later corruption, the name of Yahweh, meaning, in rough translation from the Hebrew, "I AM WHO I AM" (Ex 3:14), which St. Thomas Aquinas explained as the only being whose essence and existence are one. This leads us into deep philosophical waters, which I won't sail into right now. But you will see in the chapters ahead that the Yahweh of Scripture and Aquinas is a far, far cry from the bearded and angry Jehovah of Ellis and Dawkins. Yahweh is a God, you will see, that even modern prominent "pagan" and "atheist" philosophers have come to believe does, and must, exist!

CHAPTER 4

Aristotle Shrugged: Ayn Rand and the Intellectual Soul

"Do not let your vision of man be distorted by the ugly, the cowardly, the mindless in those who have never achieved his title. Do not lose your knowledge that man's proper estate is an upright posture, an intransigent mind and a step that travels unlimited roads."

AYN RAND, *Atlas Shrugged*[1]

"Man has a single basic choice: to think or not, and that is the gauge of his virtue. Moral virtue is an unbreached rationality — not the degree of your intelligence, but the full and relentless use of your mind, not the extent of your knowledge, but the acceptance of reason as an absolute."

AYN RAND, *Atlas Shrugged*[2]

"I would identify the sense of life dramatized in The Fountainhead *as man worship."*

AYN RAND, Introduction to *The Fountainhead*[3]

We've talked a lot about the man with biceps of steel. In this chapter, we'll focus on the shoulders of giants, both a mythical giant and a man who some would say is the biggest intellectual giant in all of human history. The first giant held up the world, while the second has shaped it like few others. Both of these giants happened to be Greek. And, yes, we'll be focusing primarily on an incomparably unique Russian (and thoroughly American) female novelist and philosopher. She stood on the shoulders of both of these giants. Please allow me to explain.

Atlas Shrugged

The Titans were a proud race of gods in ancient Greek mythology. They ran the world before they were dethroned by Zeus and his younger generation of Olympians. Zeus, it was told, assigned Atlas, one of the surviving stalwart Titans, the task of holding up the heavens. Over time, he came to be depicted holding up the Earth. (I know this for a fact, because as I look at my globe on the other side of the study, there is indeed a little bronze figure of Atlas himself, with the Earth upon his back. Antarctica is just over his left shoulder.)

The idea of Atlas has become associated with great power and responsibility, even in our modern culture. In the early decades of the 20th century, an Italian American, Angelo Siciliano (1893-1972), transformed himself from a "97-pound weakling" to "The World's Most Perfectly Developed Man," dubbing himself Charles Atlas. So, then, what has Atlas to do with Rand?

Ayn Rand (1905-1982) created a comprehensive philosophy that had no place for God. Her goal was to glorify man himself (see the third quotation at this chapter's start) and to make him as creative, achieving, and reasonable as humanly possible. Most of her philosophy was presented in the form of novels, with heroes, and some heroines, intended to personify and dramatically represent her philosophy in action. These characters were fictional ideals intended to inspire us and serve as models of perfection. Her grandest effort is the enormous thousand-plus-page epic *Atlas Shrugged*. The covers of some editions even depict the old Titan bent over, with the Earth on his shoulders (apparently just before the shrug). But why dig he shrug? The answer to this question brings us to the gist, and perhaps to some of the appeal, of Ayn Rand's novels, as well as her novel philosophy.

The Atlas in *Atlas Shrugged* represents modern-day creators, innovators, artists, philosophers, composers, business people, entrepreneurs, and producers of various stripes who essentially hold up the world through their efforts. What they shrugged were their responsibilities to the masses so eager to benefit from their achievements and, in the same breath, to damn them for those accomplishments.[4] Unlike the most widespread and influential atheistic philosophies of the 20th century — such as Marxist communism, Nazism, fascism, and various variants of socialism — Ayn Rand's Objectivism was all about *individual* rights. Rand taught that to have to work against one's will or to have one's earnings taken away and redistributed to others was a great affront to human rights and a monumental evil. No fan of big government was she!

The ultimate Atlas in *Atlas Shrugged* is a man named John Galt. Who is John Galt?[5]

Galt is an incredibly brilliant engineer who has engineered a "strike." Throughout the course of this novel, as great achiever after great achiever has disappeared from the face of the earth, we learn that the mysterious genius Galt has actually persuaded them to go away with him and stay in his utopian hideaway. Later, after chaos ensues in the geniuses' absence, and when the bureaucrats and the helpless masses come to their senses, Galt and his heroic friends emerge, Galt having delivered over the radio waves an incredibly long and detailed explanation of the Objectivistic philosophy, detailing how reason and capitalism would reign, once he and his friends returned to society on their terms. Please note the "upright posture" of this chapter's first quote. An Objectivist hero is not going to be laden with somebody else's burdens! Galt proclaimed he would not give a minute of his life to another man, and neither would he expect another man to give a minute of his life to him.

Aristotle Shrugged?

We'll get back to a more thorough description of Rand's philosophy and novels — including my personal favorite — in due course. For now, let's talk about that second Greek giant. He's the one — indeed, virtually the *only* one — to whom Rand herself declared indebtedness.

In the last chapter, I mentioned social scientist Charles Murray's book *Human Accomplishment*. When Murray cataloged the most influential thinkers of the last 2,800 years, he even went so far as to argue for *the single most influential figure in all of human history*, in terms of the arts and sciences. This man ranked not only number three in combined sciences, and number two in biology, but also number one in philosophy — a completely unparalleled achievement. This man was Aristotle (384-322 B.C.).

But what of Rand and Aristotle, and why would I have him shrugging? *The essence of Ayn Rand's allure to the young is her intoxicatingly high praise of human potential in terms of intellectual and productive achievement.* She states flat out that a man should be a hero, and that women can be heroes, too, in a sense, though women's ultimate fulfillment is in the hero-worship of the heroic man. She describes great potential for earthly joys, all based upon the full exercise of the human intellect. (This is also why "intellectual soul" is a part of this chapter's title. I'll describe it more fully when we get to the chapter on St. Thomas Aquinas.) For Rand, the key to human happiness boils down to the free and proper exercise of our abilities to think and reason. She praises Aristotle so highly because she recognizes him as the man who first and most fully recognized and laid down the fundamental laws of human intellectual functioning.

Indeed, Rand writes that, starting with the basic unquestionable logical axioms of Aristotle — such as "A is A," a thing is what it is, also known as the Law of Identity — one will eventually arrive at all of the metaphysical, ethical, political, economic, and artistic conclusions of her philosophy of Objectivism. Her system, she argues, is the full embodiment of reason: valid premises followed logically to their unarguable conclusions.

Aristotle formulated the valid laws of logical reasoning, and therefore, he was the man! And in this, I personally believe she got a great deal right.

So why is Aristotle shrugging? I don't picture him shrugging off any burdens as Atlas did. Rather, I envision him hearing Rand claim that her system was the natural outgrowth and fulfillment of his philosophy, and shrugging his shoulders as if to say, "Whatever!" Actually, though, Aristotle was anything but the "Whatever!" type. Before this book is concluded, I'll tell you why Rand's system is but the acorn and Aristotle's the mighty oak.

The Fountainhead of Achievement

Ayn Rand wrote several gripping novels. *We the Living* (1936) tells the dramatic story of heroic human beings crushed under the newly formed communist regime in Soviet Russia. *Anthem* (1938) is a brief and captivating novella about a man in a futuristic, completely socialized world of "us" and "we" who rediscovers the word "I." Around the time George Orwell was writing about the incredibly efficient, high-tech though spirit-crushing future world of *1984*, Rand wrote of similar perils, except she had the foresight to see not technological advancement, but economic and materialistic regression under a world of forced communalism and squashed individual freedoms. *Atlas Shrugged* (1957) has been briefly described, but I discovered my own personal favorite in 1981, at the age of 20. In it, Rand described the fountainhead of human achievement, that fountainhead being "man's mind" — and that book, of course, is *The Fountainhead* (1943).

"Howard Roark laughed." This is the first line of *The Fountainhead*. Howard Roark was laughing, even though he had just been kicked out of architectural school, and architecture was his life's passion. His story is only incidentally about architecture, however. Howard Roark is the man who stands on his own two feet and follows nothing but his own better judgment. He is the exact opposite of the kind of guy who does something just because everyone else is doing it. My mom used to say of my influential friends, "If so-and-so said, 'Go jump in a lake,' would you do it?" Well, Howard Roark certainly would not. (It just so happens that Roark's second action in the novel is indeed to dive into a pond — but it's his own idea!)

Howard Roark is my favorite of Rand's heroes. He is like the sheriff hero of *High Noon*, who stands alone to champion what he sees as right.[6] Howard Roark builds incredible structures based on his own ideas. He does not steal ideas from others, nor does he bow to conventions and popular fashions or opinions. He is interested in enjoying life and in achieving great things, with little interest in money for its own sake, and with no interest at all in power over others. His great friend in the novel is the very powerful and successful businessman Gail Wynand, who runs a newspaper empire. He, too, exercises his intellectual powers and stacks one achievement upon the other, but he kowtows to the lowest common denominator of the masses. He publishes not the truth, but what people want to hear, and are willing to buy. He lacks integrity, and only at the end of his life does he see Roark's moral superiority.[7]

Indeed, Rand later revealed that Wynand's character was actually quite Nietzschean. Rand was influenced by Nietzsche's boldness in her youth, and she admired his critique of altruism and self-sacrifice, but she later came to renounce him as a mystic and an irrationalist. Rand, you see, described three major forces that move mankind: (1) faith, (2) force, and (3) reason.

Faith, for Rand, was a primitive, pre-rational, and irrational way of thinking associated with religious belief. The representatives of faith include priests, theologians, and other religious types who hoodwink and control believers with their mystical mumbo-jumbo. Rand colorfully referred to them as the "witch doctors."

Force, for Rand, represented the brute force of violence and military might, exemplified, first of all, by mighty military leaders throughout history, all the way down to minor street thugs. She dubbed those who personified force as "Attilas," patterned after Attila the Hun.

Those who chose *reason* were the followers of Aristotle, until she came along. Nietzsche, to paraphrase Rand, essentially rejected "the witch doctor," but only to champion "Attila."

So Howard Roark moves along through life, mostly encountering "second-handers," people who choose not to think and live for themselves, but to let others do their thinking (and sometimes their working) for them. He stands intransigent, unbending, doing his own thing — even leading to a very controversial episode in which he dynamites a housing tenement erected in a breach of contract with him — until he ultimately gets his girl and his contract, ending in ultimate worldly success by refusing to compromise his principles. In a sense, he, too, is like "the Man of Steel," a man of steel who builds triumphant skyscrapers out of steel.

Rand Against the Atheists

Rand herself was much like Roark. She stood alone and would not bend. (For her later novels, she would not allow editors to alter a single word!) She stood out from every crowd, even from her fellow atheists. Because of her roots in Aristotle — unlike most modern atheists, agnostics, and secularists of all sorts — Ayn Rand was *not* a relativist. She did indeed believe in objective truth. That is why, of course, she called her system Objectivism. She believed in absolute right and wrong. She argued that gray is merely a mixture of black and white. We are morally responsible to pick out the truth and to reject the false in every important issue. Compromise with evil is not an option.

Rand was no fan of Albert Ellis and his lack of belief in absolutes. You may recall, from Chapter 3, his book denouncing Objectivism as a religion and later as "fascistic" and "fanatical." Her thoughts on Bertrand Russell were similar. Nietzsche, as we saw, was an irrational "Attila" to her. She largely ignored Charles Darwin.

Rand herself was no favorite of the academics or other mainstream atheists. She had written much of her philosophy in the form of fiction, after all, and she had no formal postgraduate degree in philosophy. More importantly, she was not of the collectivistic, anti-individualist, socialistic school of thought that dominated most of 20th-century atheism.

Rand was no militant atheist either, by the way. She did not fight to remove God from public schools. Indeed, she did not think it was the government's business to even be in the education business. She did not insist on saying "Happy Holidays!" She even wrote an essay on why she loved Christmas — though, indeed, it was for the materialistic, gift-exchanging part, and because of the joy it brings. After the death of her husband, I saw her admit on Phil Donahue's TV show that she wished there was a heaven. She was also willing to say "God bless you" on that show, because she considered it an expression of benevolence and goodwill.

Rand always argued that people should be judged as individuals and not as members of a particular race or ethnicity. She happened to be born into a Russian Jewish family, and her real name was Alisa Rosenbaum. Her father's pharmacy business was ruined by the Russian Revolution. She hated communism with a passion, and loved the fact that she was an American citizen by her own choice and actions. She believed in freedom and hated the inherent slavery that she saw in socialistic systems. She believed that Christianity and all religious systems denigrated the individual and man himself by declaring that there is something higher than the individual human mind. Rand's heroes always fought for what they saw as right, and they usually won.

Rand was also a champion of selfishness. Through the character of Roark in *The Fountainhead*, she said that the world was "perishing from an orgy of self-sacrifice." She wrote of love, but she treated it as a voluntary, *contractual* exchange. There is nothing that one human being *owes* to another. It is kind of like, "I see positive things in you that satisfy what I want, and you see positive things in me that satisfy your desires. All right, then, it's a deal!" Still, during a radio interview Rand was asked if there was anybody we really stood indebted to, who could really lay a claim on us, whether we liked it or not. Rand explained that we really do owe responsibilities to two people: our parents. She explained that they gave us life and cared for us when we were incapable. (It sounded suspiciously like the Fourth Commandment to me.)

In any case, Rand influenced me, and plenty of others, for decades. Because of her strong defense of individualism, capitalism, individual rights, and severely limited government, she was part of the inspiration for the Libertarian Party, was not unknown to many Reagan-era Republicans, once counted former Federal Reserve Board Chairman Alan Greenspan among her Objectivists, and was indirectly influential in the "self-esteem" movement in psychology. Though her work was held in disdain by many academics, in popular polls of Americans' favorite novels, *Atlas Shrugged* and *The Fountainhead* are often very near the top of the list. Indeed, the "Rand" name appears with other American writers on the facade of one of America's major bookstore chains.

I think Ayn Rand was quite right in giving special significance to the value of the human intellect; in championing individual rights and limiting unnecessary encroachment of freedoms by governing bodies; in praising Aristotle; in seeing fiction as a means of portraying what is best in us, and inspiring us to emulate it; and in many other things. She's had a lasting impact on me. I also believe she was very wrong in some extremely important issues, and I feel a duty to my fellowman to explain just why as this book progresses. I will not shrug it off.

TRUTH BOX #4

Vacating the Premise

"Existence exists!"[8]

Whoa, Nelly! Hold your horses. I'm not saying that existence does *not* exist. I'm just calling into question the legitimacy of the fundamental premise that led Ayn Rand to atheism.

Rand said her philosophy could be summed up in the phrase "Existence exists." She also used to love to say, "Check your premises." What I'd like to do is check *her* premise and examine whether stating "existence exists" really explains anything at all regarding *God's* existence, or the lack thereof.

Rand indicates that saying existence exits implies two inescapable axioms: (1) *existence*, there really is a world out there, and (2) *consciousness*, there is a faculty capable of perceiving existence. I think I'm with her on that. Recall the correspondence theory of truth: the correct correlation between what actually is and what we believe about it. But I also think she tries to milk the statement "existence exists" far beyond the capacity of its udders.

You see, the Objectivists jump straight to the additional premise that existence *just plain exists* — that is, existence itself is totally *self-sufficient* and needs no explanation. Here, I'm afraid that the axiom will shrug, being forced to bear a burden beyond its strength. Can we satisfactorily answer the question of *why* all that we see exists, with "It just does," and proclaim that this is an axiom that allows no further questioning?

I wonder, too, how this might relate to the question that — or so Bertrand Russell thought — dealt God the fatal blow, namely, "Who made God?" Could some kind of a fundamental misunderstanding of the concepts of existence and of God be lurking about the "premises?" Please keep reading. We'll look into this.

CHAPTER 5

Darwin and Dawkins:
Genes, Memes, and "Me's"

"Light will be thrown on the origin of man and his history."
CHARLES DARWIN, *On the Origin of Species*[1]

"Faith (belief without evidence) is a virtue. The more your beliefs defy the evidence, the more virtuous you are. Virtuoso believers who can manage to believe something really weird, unsupported and insupportable, in the teeth of evidence and reason, are especially highly rewarded."
RICHARD DAWKINS, *The God Delusion*[2]

"I won't utter falsehoods, but I've no objection to uttering meaningless statements."
RICHARDS DAWKINS, *The Four Horsemen* video[3]
(quoting another atheist in defending
why he said grace before meals)

The most prominent proselytizers of what is called the "new atheism" base their faith upon the Darwinian theory of evolution, and biologist Richard Dawkins is the most prominent among them. I suppose, then, that I, when a young man, was really an "old atheist" — that is, my atheism was based on what I thought were carefully considered philosophical arguments, rather than a blind application of scientific theories to realms beyond the reach of science. Because I had some grounding in philosophy, this current batch of new atheists could not have begun to sell me their brand of atheism, but they have a powerful influence today. For example, Dawkin's book *The God Delusion* has reportedly sold more than 1.5 million copies.

It is disconcerting to consider the effect of these atheistic writings and pronouncements on people with as little grounding in philosophy, let alone theology, as these books' scientific authors. I'll jump into that brouhaha a few pages down the road. But for now, let's start with the common ancestor from whom the current batch of atheists descended, as I provide some of my own recollections and reflections.

The Origin of My Views on Evolution

One of my first recollections of the history of the theory of evolution, aside from high school biology class, was in Philosophy 101 back in 1979. Here I learned from one text that the general idea of descent or change in species had been around long before the time of Charles Darwin (1809-1882). The ancient Greek philosopher Anaximander (611-541 B.C.), for example, theorized that life had sprung from primordial dampness and mud, and that humans had evolved over time from fish. (Arguments followed that we should abstain from eating fish, lest we devour our ancestors.) Anyway, by the time I was a college student, I had little doubt of the veracity of the modern Darwinian theory of evolution.

A decade or so later, when I first taught Life-Span Development Psychology for the University of Illinois at Springfield, we covered topics of relevance to human origins and development, both in terms of *species heredity* (the common genetic inheritance of the human race) and *individual heredity* (the inherited characteristics that make each of us unique). Our textbooks' brief summaries of Darwin's theory of evolution noted that modern evolutionary theories build upon Darwin's basic ideas:

1. Individual members of any species *vary* in what they have inherited from their parents. (We now know, unlike Darwin, that this is due to genes, and that this is the *individual heredity* that captures the differences between two different tigers, or between you and me, for example.)

2. Some of those differences are more *adaptive* than others. (For example, there are survival advantages to being smarter, stronger, or faster — widely known now as *the survival of the fittest*.)

3. Genes that aid in adaptation are more likely to allow their possessors to survive long enough to pass along those genes to their offspring (what we might call "*reproduction of the fittest*").

Therefore, gradually, over vastly long periods of time, the genetic makeup of whole species can change or evolve, becoming ever better, and more adapted to their environment. This process is termed *natural selection*.

So there you have it, very briefly. In courses on developmental psychology, we typically move on to various theories of human psychology based on the evolutionary premise that certain capacities (such as human cognition), emotions (such as empathy), and even principles (such as altruism and caring for others) — the goal being survival of the species, as well as one's self — have evolved through these natural processes. Next, we move into the workings of individual genetics (including things like the laws of inheritance, the biology of genes, chromosomes, RNA, DNA, and the like), as well as theories that measure "heritability" (for example, how likely it is that people of various degrees of biological kinship will develop the same disease or obtain similar IQ scores). This is all very fascinating stuff indeed.

So, as a professor of a topic as broad as that of human development, and like most of my peers, I would teach from a textbook providing nice compilations of the most recent theories and research in a variety of areas. This textbook material was supplemented with information gleaned from a review of several complementary copies of competing textbooks from different publishers, and spiced with a sampling of the most recent research articles that I had perused and that my students had brought to my attention via their obligatory research papers.

At the time, I was also aware of a tendency in the social sciences to focus only on the most recent research, assuming that anything written more than a few years earlier was outdated and had been superseded (a very nice tendency indeed for the publishers of academic journals). From my own experience, I was aware, however, that the best and most important work is not always that which is hottest off the press. A historical approach is also necessary for the grasp of any subject related to human behavior. Fads come and go, not only in the tabloids and celebrity magazines but in academic journals as well. In fact, I'll include an example in Chapter 8.

Furthermore, I've always been suspicious of overspecialization, and I have felt the need to supplement my area of expertise with broad-based, general study. If I was going to include the theory of evolution in my psychology classroom, then, by golly, I'd better brush up on that topic as well. Now, being a fan, at that time, of Mortimer Adler (our star of Chapter 8), I was also a big believer in the "great books." So, rather than settle for the glossiest, most up-to-date summaries of evolutionary theory, why not go to the original master, and to the great books of evolution themselves?

From Acorn to Oak to Colossus Maximus

I write this sitting behind (or within) an over-eight-foot-long oaken desk I designed for such business. At a friend's suggestion, I named it: Colossus Maximus — or Colossus, for short. It wraps partially around me, with a wing on the right that I can further extend with a pullout writing surface, which extends to the wall behind me. There is also another pullout to the left, so I can enclose myself within an oaken surface vast enough to house a slew of open books as I do my research, freshen my memory, craft my words, and try them out on you.

While Colossus has only two Spartan, little drawers, it is suffused with bookshelves. There are shelves to my immediate right, and also under the open space of the desk. And the desk connects on my left to a two-tiered bookshelf that spans the entire length of the room. The right side of the desk's exterior is also a bookshelf. The result is that I can keep many hundreds of tomes within my fingertips, and I can get at a good hundred or more without ever leaving my seat.

So what does Colossus have to do with evolution? Well, though I personally designed Colossus for my purposes — and had souls far more gifted than me actually build it — I recall with pleasant memory that it was behind the more modest confines of my first writing desk, within my first modest study, in my early 30s, that I read with great pleasure a replication of the first edition of Charles Darwin's *On the Origin of Species by Means of Natural Selection* (1859). It now sits open before me on the surface of Colossus.

Darwin was a gifted writer, producing crisp and felicitous prose understandable to the interested layman. He began by stating how his observations in South America as a naturalist aboard the H.M.S. Beagle "seemed to throw some light on the origin of species — that mystery of mysteries...."[4] He then moved from explanations of biological changes and variations under purposeful, human-guided domestication and breeding to an examination of the struggle for existence within the animal world. He proceeded to his theory of how nature itself selects adaptive variations, producing by its own hand progressive refinements and changes that produce significant changes within a species, and which even then produce new species.

Indeed, toward the end of this book, Darwin theorized that "psychology will be based on a new foundation, that of the necessary acquirement of each mental power and capacity by gradation."[5] Further, he opined that life had originally "been breathed into a few forms or into one,"[6] implying that even man had evolved from some simple primordial organism long, long ago. Indeed, he stated that "light will be thrown on the origin of man and his history,"[7] which he would later flesh out in *The Descent of Man and Selection in Relation to Sex* (1871). Darwin also wrote in *On the Origin of Species* that "as natural selection works solely by and for the good of each being, all corporeal and mental endowments will tend to progress towards perfection,"[8] and from this idea would descend... our superman!

In This Corner — Richard Dawkins; and in This Corner — God

All right, it's time to cut to the chase and bring you the main event. If we fast-forward 150 years from the publication of *On the Origin of Species* in 1859, we find, as I noted, that the new atheism is rife with Darwinists. Some very prominent scientists — mostly biologists, and most prominently Richard Dawkins — believe that Darwin's theory of evolution is true, *and* that it leaves no room for God. They have taken off the gloves and are pulling no punches. They believe that for any thinking person, the bell has wrung, the match is over, and God is dead — again!

Evolutionary biologist Richard Dawkins (b. 1941) is so certain of his beliefs in Darwinism and atheism that he is quite willing to jump into the realm of psychiatry and clinical psychology, labeling belief in God "delusional," and noting that any modern educated person who believes in God must be either insane or intellectually deficient.

In fact, Dawkins himself belongs to a group of atheists (and those with affiliated purely materialistic, naturalistic [non-spiritual] worldviews) that call themselves "Brights" — implying, I suppose, that those of us with differing opinions are a wee bit "Dim."

Well, good Dr. Dawkins, I write as a psychologist who has been licensed to diagnose mental disorders involving such phenomena as delusions, and I have actually administered hundreds of intelligence tests. I have also been a member of Mensa, the "high IQ society," and for several years served on its Research Review Committee, which presents monetary awards to researchers doing the best pioneering work on the study of human intelligence. Still, I would never presume to diagnose a person in terms of mental illness or intellectual capacity who I had never actually evaluated, let alone billions of individuals I have never met. Further, I will endeavor to try to avoid the same egregious offense to science by lecturing anyone on the truth or falsity of evolutionary biology per se, lacking the proper credentials and knowledge base in that field.

You see, whether or not evolutionary changes occur with the material bodies of living creatures is indeed a matter for science to decide. I am well aware that most modern biologists believe that Darwin's theory of natural selection, as a mechanism of evolutionary change, is the best theory. Things such as the Benedictine monk Gregor Mendel's discovery of the laws of inheritance and the later discoveries of genes and DNA were unknown to Darwin, but were in some ways predicted by his theory. The bottom line is that equating evolutionary change with a "Darwinism" that necessitates atheism is a *non sequitur* — that is, it does not logically follow. The teachings of the Catholic Church do not rule out biological evolution.

Moreover, Dawkins and God should not even be in the same ring, if it is possible that God created Dawkins, as well as the entire universe — including, of course, the ring.

We need to leave false dichotomies out of this issue. In America, for example, we have seen the story of the teaching of evolution in the schools portrayed in the media as a battle between scientists (evolution's closest approximation to mental perfection to date) and uneducated, backwoods Bible-thumpers (of questionable breeding and surely marked for extinction). Either the Earth is billions of years old and God had no role in it or God made every species just as it is today, during those six fateful days about 4,500 years ago.

This is not the full story, of course. Even 1,700 years ago, St. Augustine, bishop of Hippo in Africa, wrote that the Bible is not a textbook of science, and that it should not be interpreted in ways that are contrary to human reason. St. Thomas Aquinas was very much aware of multiple levels of causation, and that God, as the final and principal cause, gave secondary powers of causation to His creatures as well. There is nothing that would prevent God from producing a creation that would unfold itself over time. Because God is eternal and outside of time, an evolving creation would present no surprises to Him either!

Much of the explanatory power of the theory of natural selection involves the profound effects that very minimal changes can produce if vast amounts of time are allowed for the changes to accumulate. Dawkins, for example, has written many fine books explaining evolutionary theory that describe this potential process. Others have written critiques arguing that even so, and even granting billions of years for the processes of natural selection to tinker, there still has not been nearly enough time for nature to have constructed some of the complex structures of living organisms. This delves into the area of "intelligent design," which I am not going to address here. In Truth Box #11 (p. 181), however, I will offer several suggestions for further reading.

All right, let's say that life evolves from simpler species to more complex and better adapted species. This does not explain the origin of life itself, only how it changes. It also explains only material changes and cannot speak to spiritual issues. Further, if life eventually arose through the aftereffects of the big bang 13 billion years ago, then who fired it off, and where did the original matter come from? Again, in recent years, a vast genre of literature exploring such issues has arisen, to answer the atheists, and I will tip you off in Truth Box #11 to some I found most useful. There are books by biochemists and physicists that argue that their findings in no way rule out the existence of a Creator. There are also wonderful books by philosophers and theologians who address the philosophical and theological naiveté of Dawkins and the other new atheists. I don't want to walk over their ground again. What I would like to do is provide a few of my own recollections and reflections on the non sequiturs and false dichotomies of the new atheists from the perspective of a doctor of psychology.

What Do God, Fairies, and Santa Claus Have in Common?

The new atheists' answer, of course, is that all of them are fictional, and that none of them actually exist as anything more than ideas at best and "delusions" at worst. The examples of fairies and Santa Claus were used by Albert Ellis (Chapter 3). As we saw in Truth Box #3 (see p. 67), Ellis, like Dawkins, did not believe in absolute certainty, and said he could not say he was *certain* God does not exist, but that the probability that He does exist is "exactly the same degree" as the probability that applies to Santa Claus and fairies — yes, he says "exactly the same degree"![9] Richard Dawkins stands in agreement and uses similar examples.

This is a very intriguing proposition when we consider how many of the greatest philosophical and scientific geniuses in all of humanity, throughout history, and even today, do believe in God. We can only wonder: Did Aristotle hope that little elves would come and tidy up the Lyceum during the night? Did St. Augustine stay up late to sneak a peek at Santa? I haven't the temerity to e-mail Francis Collins — a professing Christian and head of the Human Genome Project — to inquire whether or not he has dreamed of sequencing the DNA of the Easter Bunny, or to e-mail Antony Flew, world-renowned atheistic philosopher turned theist, to see if perhaps leprechauns really persuaded him to change his mind, and not the rule of Socrates, to follow wherever the argument leads.

Of course, I'm being facetious here, but please bear in mind that the new atheists are not. *How grand it must be to so confidently declare that the profound questions which so taxed the greatest minds in human history are mere child's play for one's own!*

And here is one place that a little psychology may come into play. Dawkins believes that religious believers are acting like babies, with their infantile beliefs in a God with no more plausibility than the tooth fairy. Some have argued that Dawkins sets up and knocks down straw men in his attacks on religion. He has defined faith, for example, as "blind trust, in the absence of evidence, even in the teeth of evidence."[10] We will see later — in our examination of St. Thomas Aquinas in Chapter 9 and Pope John Paul II in Chapter 12 — a Catholic interpretation of the relationship between faith and reason.

Still, I don't fully agree with the straw man charge. Dawkins sets up not straw men, but *straw babies*, though he certainly denies it, stating:

I know you don't believe in an old bearded man sitting on a cloud, so let's not waste any more time on that. I am attacking God, all gods, anything and everything supernatural, wherever and whenever they have been or will be invented.[11]

With Santa Claus, "fairies at the bottom of the garden,"[12] and God all occupying similar places in Dawkins's Easter basket, I question not just his interpretation of the writings of theologians, but whether he has even heard of modern scientific psychological research on the development of religious beliefs over the course of an individual's lifespan.

Psychologist James Fowler, for example, produced an empirical, evidence-based theory of the stages of faith development. In *Stages of Faith*[13] and in other writings, he detailed his findings based on interviews with individuals from age 3 to 84. He found that as we mature and develop, from early childhood toward the end of life, there is a common and predictable course of increasing abstraction and sophistication in one's faith that parallels the growth in cognitive abilities demonstrated by psychologist Jean Piaget and the growth in moral development documented by psychologist Lawrence Kohlberg.

Indeed, through the early and later childhood years, during stages of *intuitive-projective* and *mythic-literal* faith, we commonly find very simple and concrete beliefs. Here we do find that kindly, old bearded God, resting upon His cloud. However, by the time we reach adolescence, and our abilities to think abstractly have blossomed, we see *synthetic-conventional* faith, in which religious beliefs become organized and synthesized into coherent systems of belief, usually meshing with those of one's family or influential peers.

In early adulthood, some individuals will begin to question and to think deeply about their religious beliefs during the stage of *individuative-reflective* faith. This is especially common when they have encountered life experiences that may challenge their beliefs (perhaps in their college courses). As they search for a belief system that makes sense to them, they may reject some or all of their prior beliefs, as happened to me. Some will experience the stage of *conjunctive faith* in middle age, in which understanding deepens — for example, the capacity to make sense of paradoxes, such as, perhaps, the presence of suffering when God is all-loving. Finally, a rare few may attain the highest stage of *universalizing faith*, in which one achieves a sense of oneness with being and of universal love. One of Fowler's examples was Mother Teresa of Calcutta.

Hence, I maintain that Dawkins is indeed attacking the straw-baby God of childhood faith when he considers belief in God an exact parallel to belief in fairies at the bottom of the well, a "cosmic teapot"[14] orbiting our sun (borrowing here from Bertrand Russell), and even "The Flying Spaghetti Monster."[15]

Next, let's take a look at what Dawkins himself believes, not only about God but also faith itself, and about some very interesting hypothetical constructs of his own.

Faith in the Teeth of the Evidence

Please review, if you will, Dr. Dawkins's first quotation at the beginning of this chapter.

Now, if (a) faith is a virtue and (b) faith means belief without evidence and (c) the "weirder" the thing one believes "in the teeth of the evidence," the more virtuous one is, then (d) we shall see that Dr. Dawkins himself is indeed a most faithful and virtuous scientist.[16] Indeed, if we but have faith in Dr. Dawkins's Darwinistic view, *not only of the evolution of biological forms, but of the origin and purpose* (well, actually, lack of purpose) *of the whole universe*, then we, too, shall be able to believe in such things as:

- **Memes:** Units of culture varying from things like a snippet of a song to grand political or religious ideas that are spread throughout humanity by imitation. Dawkins explains religion as a virus-like by-product of natural selection.
- **Memeplexes:** "Sets of memes" that survive in the presence of other members of memeplexes, even though they themselves may not aid survival.
- **Memeticists:** Experts in the study of memes and memeplexes.
- **Multiple universes:** These are universes that "survive" and "reproduce within black holes," passing on their inherited characteristics and mutations to "daughter universes," some of which then survive and, if lucky enough to produce enough black holes, spawn yet more universes — our own, of course, being one of them. (What is the evidence? Well, we're here, aren't we? Check *The God Delusion* if you don't believe me.[17])

If you have faith in this Darwinian view of the entire universe (excuse me, *universes*), you will also obtain the capacities to:

- Teach theologians about theology.
- Teach biblical scholars about the Bible.
- Teach physicists about physics.
- Give Aristotle lessons in logic, metaphysics, and ethics.
- Enlighten psychiatrists and clinical psychologists about delusions and the workings of the mind.
- Save psychometricians time in searching for mysterious missing IQ points on the test profiles of the religious.

I'll address all this meme business in the next section. For now, let me note that *The God Delusion* is rife with the marvelous achievements made possible by Dawkins's own faith in his particular view of science. For example, biologist Dawkins tells us he can understand and appreciate theories like those of multiple universes, or a "megaverse," though "the idea is hated by most physicists." Why? Dawkins answers, "A mischievous biologist might wonder whether some other physicists are in need of Darwinian consciousness raising."[18] Throughout Dawkins's writings on religion, he is extremely careful to use only extreme examples that bolster his idiosyncratic definition of faith and its role in relation to reason. He enlightens us with several lines from Martin Luther on the relationship of faith and reason: for example, "Reason is the greatest enemy that faith has; it never comes to the aid of spiritual things, but more frequently than not struggles against the divine Word...."[19] He does not note, however, that Luther was no fan of St. Thomas Aquinas, a thinker of the very first rank who had written centuries before Luther that "human reason does not exclude the merit of faith but is a sign of greater merit."[20]

And speaking of reason, let's move right along to the related concept of human intellectual capacities. When Swiss psychologist Jean Piaget produced the most thoroughly tested theory of the development of human cognition, his highest stage of "formal operational reasoning" was characterized by the ability to mentally manipulate not only concrete things, but abstract ideas as well. When modern psychologists have been polled on the defining characteristic of human intelligence, the number one choice again and again has been "abstract reasoning" abilities. These abilities are what clearly separate the adult from the child, and all the more, human beings from the lower animals. Indeed, these capacities characterize the uniquely human "rational soul" described by Aristotle and Aquinas millennia ago.

And indeed, there are also *individual differences* between people in the powers of these abstract-reasoning capacities. In the last 100 years, IQ tests were developed to measure these capacities to predict how people will perform in various settings, such as the schoolroom and the workforce. Let's see what theologian St. Thomas Aquinas opined on the matter in the 13th century: "Experience shows that some understand more profoundly than do others; as one who carries a conclusion to its first principles and ultimate causes understands it better than one who reduces it to its proximate causes."[21] So, again, a hallmark of human intelligence is the capacity to reason abstractly *from*, and *not contrary to*, or "in the teeth of," the evidence of concrete things we can detect with our senses — and according to St. Thomas, faith and reason point to the same truths. They do not lead to contradictory answers.

Dawkins speaks of belief in God as something for the uneducated and unintelligent. Indeed, in one passage he brings up the hypothetical guilt-ridden Roman Catholic "possessed of normal human frailty and less than normal intelligence."[22] He also cites a "meta-analysis" combining the results of many psychological research studies that showed that religious belief was inversely proportional to intelligence and educational level (i.e., the more intelligent/educated one is, the less likely one is to report religious belief).

Dawkins notes that this study was reported in the *Mensa Bulletin* in 2002, that Mensa is the high IQ society, and that "their journal not surprisingly includes articles on the one thing that draws them together."[23] Well, their *journal* does indeed focus on theoretical and research articles on human intelligence, and it is called the *Mensa Research Journal*. I'm aware of this because in that same year, I wrote a review of *The International Handbook of Giftedness and Talent* (second edition) for it.[24]

Now, the *Mensa Bulletin* is a publication that goes out to all Mensa members, and it certainly does address issues of intelligence. But while it is not a scholarly research journal, it does address all kinds of other things, and has many times published articles and letters on the subjects of religion and atheism. Indeed, the members — all with IQs of at least 130, the top 2 percent of the population — hold a great variety of opinions on things theological.

American Mensa also has an Education and Research Foundation that includes a Research Review Committee. That committee reviews, grades, and bestows awards every year to exemplary scientific researchers who publish academic articles on human intelligence. And I have it on good authority that at least one of their own committee members reverted from atheism to theism — in fact, to Roman Catholicism, in 2004. (I know that for certain, of course, because that member is me.)

Personal anecdotes aside, one of the most fundamental lessons that psychology professors teach their students in their very first lecture on social science research is the simple fact that *correlation does not prove causation.* Any weak (or even strong, for that matter) tendency for higher intelligence or higher levels of education to be found among the less religious in some modern studies does not "prove" that their intellectual capacity or educational attainment is the "cause" of irreligion — in the sense that the smarter you are, the less likely you are to be hoodwinked by irrational religious arguments, which is the clear implication of those who cite such studies.

In terms of educational attainment, *what the students are being taught* might also have a great influence on their religious beliefs or lack thereof. When the Catholic Church created the university system in Europe in medieval times, the correlation may have been different. Further, perhaps with higher measured intelligence comes a greater likelihood of intellectual "hubris," or pride, inclining one to assume that he knows a little more than he really does — indeed, even more than the greatest minds in human history for millennia before him.

Plato told us that an ancient oracle declared Socrates to be the wisest man in Athens. They didn't have IQ tests back then, of course, but that old theistic stonemason was considered the wisest among them because he realized that he knew so little. Of course, silly old Socrates had not had his consciousness raised by Darwinism.

Me, Myself, and Memes

Perhaps one of the weirdest of Dawkins's own brainchildren, if not "mind viruses," is the concept of the *meme*. It struck me as rather absurd even in my halcyon days of mature atheism. Indeed, in 1999, I had attended a meeting of the local skeptics society, the Rational Examination Association of Lincoln Land. They were not particularly interested in religious topics, but focused mostly on debunking claims of the paranormal in the name of reason and science. One night, I had attended a showing of a video of Dr. Susan Blackmore, who was promoting the ideas behind her book *The Meme Machine*,[25] which built upon Dawkins's theory of memes. Dawkins wrote the foreword to her book, and her work is cited approvingly in *The God Delusion*. Dawkins reports that "she repeatedly visualizes a world full of brains (or other receptacles or conduits, such as computers or radio frequency bands) and memes jostling to occupy them. As with genes in a gene pool, the memes that prevail will be the ones that are good at getting themselves copied."[26]

Well, this meme business seems to me a textbook example of *reification* — treating an abstract idea as if it were a material thing. And what I find especially absurd and self-contradictory about the meme idea is that memes are believed to rule out (1) free will and (2) the self.

As for free will, Dr. Blackmore noted that she had given up the belief in free will over 20 years ago. If so, by her own reasoning, she did not freely choose to give it up. The memes denying free will in her brain must have simply come to out-number or conquer the pro-free-will memes. Why should we subscribe to the judgments of her memes over our own?

Dr. Blackmore is also an atheist, yet in her video she endorsed religious training for the young.[27] She argued that when children are exposed to multiple systems of belief, they may find absurdities and contradictions which will lead them *away from* religion. Is she not endorsing the common sense idea that when exposed to a variety of alternatives, we possess the capacity to exercise our reason and choose among them? And isn't this capacity for choice a great example of what we mean by free will?

As for the sense of a "self" or an "I" that every one of us possesses, Dr. Blackmore regards it as a meme-induced illusion. But certainly, then, this raises the question of just who or what the memes are deluding! Dawkins, Blackmore, and the rest of the meme dream team argue that their conclusions are always based on the evidence. Well, thus far, I believe there is a lot more evidence for "me's" than for "memes." Dare I say, it is *"self*-evident"?

Dawkins's Scientist Superman

Following Dawkins's reasoning, we should indeed find supermen on the horizon, as our species continues to evolve. But the closest thing we have today is the man who stands over other men by the virtue of his "consciousness raised by Darwin." Modern scientific supermen have indeed given us x-ray vision, heat rays, jets that fly faster than a speeding bullet, forces far more powerful than a locomotive, and much more. But where does the scientific superman stand in regard to truth and justice, if God himself is his kryptonite? Religion, to Dawkins and his brethren in arms, is no mere harmless delusion, but an absolute scourge to mankind. I won't begin to address it all here, but Dawkins's insistence that religious education is a form of child abuse should give some evidence of this stance.

Of course, many proclaimed God dead millennia before the "new atheists," based on the science and philosophy of their own age. Still others have believed God to be not a harmful delusion, but a useful "fictive goal." Some have denied the many gods of their own culture, capturing a glimpse of a greater single, universal God. Some have denied both the "god of the philosophers" and "the God of Abraham, Isaac, and Jacob," and then been surprised to find Him. Let's see next how another psychologist, three philosophers, and a psychologist/philosopher helped me detect some of God's vital signs.

TRUTH BOX #5

An Ignorant Atheism

The acceptance of a Darwinian materialism rejects our Western tradition of faith and religious superstition in favor of our Western tradition of reason and the empirical investigation of the world.

Dawkins and other new atheists definitely imply this untruth, that it's a matter of the enlightened scientist versus the benighted Bible-thumper! But, no, it's not! Okay, I'm sitting behind Colossus again. Across the room from my Atlas globe is one of my favorite paintings, *The School of Athens*, by the Renaissance artist Raphael (1483-1520). Smack dab in the center stand the philosopher Plato and his most brilliant student, Aristotle. Indeed, someone once said that

Plato asked all of the great questions of philosophy, and that Aristotle answered them.

Anyway, Plato is shown with his right index finger pointing upwards toward the heavens, and Aristotle is shown with his right hand held out at about waist level. Plato believed in God and in the actual reality of ideas or "forms." Aristotle also believed in God, but he held that our knowledge starts with the earth, with the evidence of our senses, which then may lead us up to the highest branch of knowledge, that of metaphysics, or natural theology, which entails the study of God.

The materialistic new atheists, you see, do battle not only with Jerusalem, as seen through the eyes of fundamentalists, but with Athens, as seen through the eyes of profound theologians. The Catholic faith has been enriched with deep philosophical insights from Plato, derived largely through the brilliant mind of St. Augustine, and with the logic and wisdom of Aristotle, as illuminated by the mind of St. Thomas Aquinas. The new atheists, and not the Catholic Church, are at war with the best of classical Western philosophy. (Would that they showed evidence of reading some!)

PART II

Signs of Life

"Philosophy has the single task of discovering the truth about the divine and human worlds. The religious conscience, the sense of duty, justice and all the rest of the close-knit, interdependent 'company of virtues,' never leave her side. Philosophy has taught men to worship what is divine, to love what is human, telling us that with the gods belong authority, and among human beings fellowship."

SENECA, *Letter 90*[1]

CHAPTER 6

Alfred Adler and the Fictive Goal of God

"The important thing is not what one is born with, but what use one makes of that equipment."

ALFRED ADLER[1]

"To hear, see, or speak, 'correctly,' means to lose one's self completely in another or in a situation, to become identified with him or with it. The capacity for identification, which alone makes us capable of friendship, love of mankind, sympathy, occupation, and love, is the basis of social interest and can be practiced and exercised only in conjunction with others."

ALFRED ADLER[2]

"Whether the highest effective goal is called God or Socialism or, as we call it, the pure idea of social interest, it always reflects the same ruling, completion-promising, grace-giving goal of overcoming."

ALFRED ADLER[3]

My decision to enroll in a doctoral program through the Adler School of Professional Psychology in Chicago was a bit of a roll of the dice. I was 31 years old, had a good job of seven years, was poised soon for a promotion, and our second son was all of two months old. Still, my employer, the State of Illinois, had made the prospect as easy as it could possibly be, having contracted with the Adler School to provide most of the courses locally, in Springfield, our state capital and our home. And so, Kathy and I decided to declare, as did Julius Caesar when crossing the Rubicon River to commence a civil war: "Ανερρίφθω κύβος" (*anerriphtho kybos*), "The die is cast."[4]

I was still apprehensive, though. For one thing, I wasn't sure about this "Alfred Adler" guy. I already had a master's degree in general psychology, with an emphasis on human cognitive development. My allegiance in the field of psychotherapy lay with the cognitive folks like Albert Ellis, whom we have already encountered, along with Aaron Beck and others of the cognitive therapy field. My first thoughts of Adler took me back to the three major "psychoanalysts": Freud, Jung, and Adler. Quick summaries of Adler's theories had emphasized things like striving for power à la Nietzsche, rather than sex à la Freud, as well as interesting, but hardly profound (to me anyway) theories like the importance of birth order in determining one's personality traits. What kind of a Rubicon was I wading into?

Fortunately, in my very first class session, by the fourth time Dr. Silverman had literally cast the dice, I knew I had backed a winner! You see, in the very first moments of the very first class, our professor had shown us a handsome little box, from which he withdrew an ordinary pair of dice. He rolled them on the table, with all of us intently staring at their paths. When they stopped, he asked us in great earnestness, "Why did they roll like that? Why didn't they float in the air?"

Someone said something to the effect that the material they are made of is heavier than air. Dr. Silverman liked that answer.

"Yes, *what these dice are made of* made them roll like that," he agreed. "But wait a minute — why did they just roll a few feet? How come they're still not rolling?"

Someone shot back something about the effect of *their shape*. They aren't round like balls, so their squared edges produced friction and slowed them down.

"Oh yes, indeed," said the professor, "their shape made them roll like that. Excellent! But wait a minute. Why did they roll at all?"

Someone answered that *the motion of his arm* is what imparted the motion in them. (Professor Silverman had thrown, or cast, the darn things, for goodness sake!)

"How silly of me," he said. "You are right. They were propelled by the motion of my own arm. Brilliant!"

The professor then had us observe while he intently peered at the dice. After a moment, he asked us, "Hey, how come these dice are *not* rolling now?"

No one offered an answer. He patiently peered around the silent room. Now, I was not the type to make a peep in a classroom. In this case, though, I decided to raise my hand and give it a try.

"Because you didn't want them to." He asked me to repeat it, which I did.

"Yes," Dr. Silverman exclaimed, "they just sat there this time because I did not want them to roll!"

So what was the point, and how did I know the answer? Well, I knew the answer because of my familiarity with another Dr. Adler — Dr. Mortimer Adler — whom we will meet two chapters down the road. Mortimer Adler knew it because he learned it from a much older professor, Aristotle of Stagira (384-322 B.C.), to be exact.

What Dr. Silverman had illustrated for us were Aristotle's classic "four causes" of events in the world. Since you were not there to see the table the professor used to roll those dice, how about I provide us with a "table" of our own?

The Four Causes		
QUESTION	CAUSE	DEFINITION
What is it made of?	**Material** cause	That *out of which* something is made.
Who or what made it?	**Efficient** cause	That *by which* something is made.
What is it being made into?	**Formal** cause	That *into which* something is made.
What is it being made for?	**Final** Cause	That *for the sake of which* something is made.

So, getting back to our simple dice, they are (a) made *out of* plastic of a certain density (material cause); (b) made *by* the dice makers and made to roll by Dr. Silverman or any dice purchaser or user (efficient cause); (c) shaped as they are with the six sides, dots, etc., so that they will *become* roll-able dice (formal cause); and (d) they roll on their course toward snake eyes, boxcars, or whatever the case might be, by Dr. Silverman or whoever rolls them *for the sake of* games of chance, or even for the sake of illustrating Aristotelian causation (final cause).

And why was this important to Alfred Adler and to modern psychologists? Well, much of modern psychology focuses on the first three causes, while ignoring the last:

- **Material Causation:** We strive to get at material causation of human behavior by examining the nature of the brain, the structure of neurons, their chemical and electrical systems of information exchange, etc. Much of modern psychiatry is focused at this material level.
- **Efficient Causation:** Today, in some theories, the "who" has completely dropped out of the causation

of human behavior, if we refer to the Ultimate Who, Who got the whole ball rolling, (more on that in the chapter on St. Thomas Aquinas). But even at the human level, we have seen how Dawkins and others have tried to remove the self as a source of efficient causation, assuming that random environmental and chemical interactions determine our behaviors in a chain of intertwined events reaching back forever.

- **Formal Causation:** Why are humans formed as we are, and where are we heading? We have seen that the Darwinians and Nietzscheans have some strong ideas on where we have come from, how it came that we are configured as we are today, and where we have been heading.

- **Final Causation:** This is the cause that some would banish from science in general, and even from the science and philosophy of the human mind. Atheistic Darwinists reject a grand purpose in the universe, and they also deny free will. Our behaviors do not derive from a *for the sake of which* in the future, they argue, but from a *because of which* — random chance events shaped through natural selection in the past.

This simple illustration was the first indication I had seen that, regarding the psychological theories of Alfred Adler, I'd rolled the lucky seven. Adler, you see, said that human behavior is not nearly so much *pushed by our past experiences* as determinists would have it; rather, much more so, we are *pulled by our goals for the future.* This view is in line not with determinism, but with *teleology* — *telos* being Greek for goal or end or purpose, the *final cause* of that "for the sake of which."

Indeed, I would soon come across Adler's general theoretical views laid side by side with those of other major theorists, such as Freudian, behavioristic, and kindred theorists. Those folks did things like deny the existence of the soul, minimize the roles of the self and consciousness, atomize or reduce complex behaviors and experiences into parts, focus on stimuli and responses, and believe all behaviors are determined from the outside by past events.

Alder stood on the opposite side of the line. He stood in company with those who gave psychology a soul, saw the self as central, took a holistic approach, and focused on what goes on inside the human mind between the stimulus and the response. Most importantly, he held that to some extent we can shape and mold ourselves through the decisions we make and the goals we choose to pursue. All this fit with my own conclusions based on my previous studies in philosophy and psychology — and though at that time in my life I did not think I could thank God for it, I should have!

Many Thanks to Good Dr. Adler, too

Though I had not returned to a belief in God by the time I completed my doctorate in clinical psychology in the fall of 1997, I had learned a great deal that could help me understand and help myself and others, and it was very good groundwork for my later return to the highest and most final of all final causes. I'll begin with a few anecdotes on good Dr. Alfred, and briefly highlight some of his wonderful insights into human psychology, before we get into the theological.

Dr. Adler himself (1870-1937) had passed away decades before my classmates and I enrolled in the graduate school bearing his name and teaching his methods. Born in Vienna, Austria, and a contemporary of Freud, he first studied ophthalmology and later moved into psychiatry. He was a somewhat portly, grandfatherly figure who loved to go to the movies for entertainment. Virtually all who knew him sung his praises as a kind and gifted individual.

Alder was very quick-witted, and also quite humble. When teaching my college classes about the psychology of vocational choice, I used to tell the following story of his amazing grasp of human nature.

A young man once came up to Dr. Adler after a talk. He explained to the great psychiatrist that he had been unable to decide upon a career after years of diligent investigation about one possible vocation after another. Could Dr. Adler tell him what he should do? Sure enough, Adler told him on the spot that he knew what he should do: he should become a career counselor, helping others examine and make choices regarding the professions they should pursue. And the man did it! Indeed, his name was Heinz Ansbacher. He later became a clinical psychologist and compiled the classic Adlerian textbook, *The Individual Psychology of Alfred Adler.*

And as for that humility, Adler would frequently make public appearances where people would present a case study of a psychologically troubled individual, after which Adler would give his impression on the likely dynamics and prescription for therapy. After laying out his ingenious impressions, though, he would characteristically conclude with a phrase that translates from the German as "Of course, everything could also be different!" Now there is humility. If only some modern psychiatrists, psychologists, and biologists would admit the same. I will confess that I liked Adler's humble little caveat or disclaimer so much that at the very end of one of my essays for the written examination at the Adler School, I concluded with Adler's line in the German — and they still passed me!

Here now is a rapid-fire rendering of some of Adler's truly great ideas that have had a lasting influence on me.

He called his system "*Individual Psychology*," not because he was focused on the individual rather than on the community, but because he saw human persons as undividable, or indivisible.

Our personalities hang together in a whole that he called the "*lifestyle.*" This concept — that everything we do reflects our "lifestyle," our fundamental ways of seeing, interpreting, feeling, and acting in the world — goes way, way back. It is seen in the writings of Aristotle and St. Augustine, how the very way we stand and move and dress and speak expresses who we are inside.

The lifestyle is largely built during childhood, though we can modify it with diligent efforts in adulthood, and it is reflected in our *early recollections,* those early childhood memories that I brought up in the Introduction. Freud's earliest recollections, for example, include a dream wherein he was very angry and urinated on his father's bed (dreams and father hatred both being among the things for which he was later famous). Carl Jung's earliest recollections include images of a funeral profession and a priest who he thought looked like a woman (religious symbols and masculinity/femininity issues being among Jung's most favored topics).

When I had to give my own early recollections as part of a class, one of mine featured — you guessed it — Superman. You see, as a 5- or 6-year-old, I had a Superman contest with a neighbor's grandson who was visiting from out of town. He came back later in blue shirt and red towel, when, of course, I appeared in full official Superman regalia. When examining early recollections, you are also to focus on the most vivid moment, and how you felt, because these can reflect the lessons you learned from the incident. I recall the other guy's look of disappointment, and my own feeling that I'd cheated. My lesson was that this kind of behavior was not very Superman-like. The true Man of Steel does not need to make anyone else feel bad to feel good about himself. His job is to uplift, not to put down!

Another excellent concept from Adler is that of the "*creative self.*" Though we certainly do not actually create ourselves (only God can do that), we do have some say in how we mold and shape ourselves. Heredity and environment, "nature and nurture," are not the be-all and end-all of what we are. They are the bricks and mortar that we use to build ourselves. Each one of us certainly has inborn individual strengths and weaknesses in mind and body — so what are we going to do about them? Each one of us is certainly influenced by our environment, by the company we keep, and by the media — so what kind of environment are we going to place ourselves in, what company shall we keep, and what media shall we watch, listen to, or read? Or as Shakespeare's Cassius says in *Julius Caesar*: "The fault, dear Brutus, is not in our stars, but in ourselves, that we are underlings."[5] (But we need not choose to be underlings.)

But what should we choose? Here, too, Dr. Adler is most helpful. As we come into the world — so small, weak, and dependent on others — one of our fundamental strivings is to become more powerful, capable, and independent. This, then, is a fundamental "vertical," or upward, striving that Adler called the "*striving for superiority*." Note well that this does not necessarily imply superiority *over others*, but actually an improvement over our previous capacities.

Adler also truly takes a holistic approach to human psychology, seeing us as mind/body unities. Some people are born with real or perceived "*organ inferiorities*" or physical weaknesses, which they then set out to overcome in one way or another. If their means to improve are mistaken, they may develop an "*inferiority complex*" and walk around with a perpetual chip on their shoulder, and possibly develop a mental disorder. If their means are good ones, they may achieve great things despite their weakness. A classic example was the stuttering Demosthenes, who trained himself to speak aloud with a mouthful of pebbles, and later became the greatest Greek orator. Adler himself once had an office situated near a circus, and he came to find that many a circus strongman had been a scrawny little kid (much like Mac, the poor lad from the comic book ads who had sand kicked in his face before he discovered Charles Atlas's muscle-building system).

So how do we determine which are good means for overcoming feelings of inferiority and which are not? What Adler later considered his most important psychological principle was that of "*social interest*," a sense of community, benevolence, and rootedness with our fellow man. These have been called "horizontal," or "outward," strivings. Striving for superiority leads to mental health when those strivings are in line with social interest — and it leads to maladjustment, and sometimes worse, when the individual becomes guided by his own idiosyncratic "private logic" that defies common sense and the desire for the good of one's fellow man. In the worst-case scenario, a person with a huge sense of inferiority may *overcompensate* with a *superiority complex*, in which he employs his own strained private logic to place others in an inferior position and consider them unworthy of his social interest. (By the way, Adler died before the atrocities of World War II, many of which were brought about courtesy of the author of the very idiosyncratic *Mein Kampf*.)

Now a couple of concluding wonderful Adlerian concepts and we're off to theology.

Adler was a great champion of the family. Our lifestyles are formed in our first years, and in large part it is our parents who prepare us to face society. They do this best by loving us, and by letting us face the natural and logical consequences of our actions through the avoidance of unnecessary pampering (and if not avoided, such pampering can also lead us to a sense of inability or unwillingness to pull our weight in helping others). Further, Adler described three main "*tasks of life*" — those being love, work, and friendship.

For Adler, then, a healthy, happy individual has set goals for himself, to build himself into the kind of person who can confidently find a spouse, live in a loving, enduring monogamous relationship, raise a family, do productive work, and reach out to friends in love. Indeed, those are tasks worth tackling. But what about God?

The Fictive Goal of God?

Now we move on to this business of "*fictive goals*" and God. Adler was strongly influenced by a contemporary philosopher, Hans Vaihinger, author of *The Philosophy of As If*, who, in turn, had been influenced by the philosophies of Immanuel Kant and Nietzsche.

In a nutshell, Adler argued that we create "fictive," or unreal, imagined goals out of our subjective experience, and that these goals then direct our "strivings" to attain them. To Adler, God was "a concretization of the idea of perfection, greatness and superiority, which has been obvious in man's thinking and feeling since time immemorial."[6]

Adler himself was born Jewish and converted to Protestantism in adulthood. Still, for Adler, God was ultimately man's *idea* of the ultimate. Unlike many modern atheists, though, Adler believed that God was a very good idea! And while he considered himself scientific, rather than religious, he sought dialogue with religious leaders and considered Christianity an ally in leading man toward social interest.

Adler essentially took Jesus' Great Commandment to love God with all our heart and our neighbor as our self as a helpful, practical guide to merely the second part — the love of neighbor, as expressed in his most fundamental principle of "social interest." Hence, God — like Nietzsche's superman, or maybe even DC Comic's Superman — was seen as a fictional model of excellence, in this case far superior to the supermen! God, however, was not perceived as necessary, as can be seen in the last quotation at the beginning of this chapter, where he indicates that the highest goal might be called God — or socialism. Witness God's interchangeability with socialism (which Adler endorsed throughout much of his career), or with Adler's own concept of social interest.

Adler was quite taken by the evolutionary ideas and theories of scientific progress so rampant in his day. In answering a Lutheran minister who argued that we attain strength for idealism only through faith (in God), Adler noted that "we would have to add that faith in science and its progress can also lend such strength."[7] (No doubt, to speak of "*faith* in science" would rankle the new atheists!)

In my own personal journey through the realms of science and religion, faith and reason, I'll note that Adler's views did temper my Randian views a bit and made me a little more receptive to the idea of faith several years down the road. Rand, remember, equated faith with mindless mysticism and the realm of the deceptive and self-serving "witch doctors." Adler saw faith as one means to the end of mental health and human welfare. Rand glorified one's own reason and blatant self-interest. Adler emphasized how our own "private logic" or idiosyncratic reasoning can lead us far astray, if it is not aligned with higher goals of other-interest (i.e., social interest).

(Coincidentally, during the time I became immersed in Adler's thought, I had two young children in my household. I found that it is very difficult to uphold *self*-interest as one's highest value — à la Rand — when you are being stared at by a little creature sitting on your lap whom you helped bring into the world. Rand had no children, by the way.)

Adler wrote that our dreams give us emotional energy to act on our goals when awake. One dream I had at this time was about one of my young sons who did not always promptly respond to parental instruction. In it, I would open a door to the kitchen and see him there with a full-grown lion at the other end of the room. My son would not respond to my gestures to come to me, so I knew I must go in and get him. This is a choice a self-respecting Objectivist should not make, though it would not be out of character for an Adlerian, and even less so for a Christian — considering, for example, the early Christians who faced real-live lions for a God they saw as far more than a "fictive goal."

Here's another note on Adler and religion that has some practical value. Adler sometimes disputed with Christian therapists on the role of guilt, remorse, and pangs of conscience. One Adlerian definition of guilt was "feelings of remorse that one does not really have." What's that all about?

The idea is that if you *really* feel guilty, you won't just mope around or complain about it. You will take some action to make things right — and that does make sense. I don't think the Adlerians who hold this view do justice to the Catholic conception of guilt, though, nor to the very special way God has given us to deal with it.

The Sacrament of Penance and Reconciliation requires *contrition* (feelings of remorse we really do have for offending God or neighbor), *confession* (admitting aloud our sins to the confessor), and *satisfaction* (actions prescribed by the priest to make amends for our sins). Clearly, the Catholic conception of sin, guilt, and what we do about it goes far beyond muttering empty phrases. Our guilt is a motivator to make the most of our actions, keeping them in line with social interest, and with God's desire for our spiritual perfection.

There is one more helpful Adlerian concept that ties into good Christian ethics. Adler noted that individuals who develop mental disorders through erroneous private logic and "mistaken" lifestyles — rather than developing a sense of social interest and cooperation with others — usually end up "putting others in their service." In other words, feelings of inferiority that express themselves in feelings of depression, anxiety, or anger often result in forcing those around the depressed, anxious, or angry person to bend to his will and care for, reassure, or submit to his demands or requests. Satan's famous reply to God, of course, was *"Non serviam!"* ("I will not serve").

When we fail to develop social interest, we end up telling others, if not in our words, then in our actions, "Serve me!"

TRUTH BOX #6

A Fictional God?

Everyone has his own unique image of God.

In describing God as an ultimate fictional goal, Adler wrote that "each individual, in a thousandfold variation, forms an image of the functioning and shape of the supreme being which differs by nuances from that of the next man.... No wonder that in the millionfold diversity of concretization the scale ranges all the way from personification to its opposite...."[8] In other words, each man crafts God in his own image (or is it really the other way around?).

In *The Case for a Creator*[9] (2004), journalist Lee Strobel summarizes his findings from discussions with modern philosophers, theologians, biologists, biochemists, physicists, psychologists, and astronomers, with a list of fundamental attributes of God consistent with both science and the Bible, which includes God as: Creator, Unique, Uncaused and Timeless, Immaterial, Personal, with Freedom of Will, Intelligent and Rational, Enormously Powerful, Creative, Caring, Omnipresent, Purpose-Giver for Humanity, and

Provider of Life After Death. Minor differences aside, these are some pretty important common conceptions of God shared by Christians.

All of these attributes are discussed in St. Thomas Aquinas's *Summa Theologica*, written 750 years ago, wherein Jesus Christ is shown as the incarnation, or "being made flesh," of this great God. So, although each man may have his own image of God, it is important to bear in mind that our images are *true* ones to the degree that they correspond to objective reality, reality as revealed to us by the working of our minds on the data from our senses and as revealed to us directly through God's revelation, and interpreted by the Church, with the Holy Spirit's guidance. And lest we forget, the Bible itself tells us that "the pillar and bulwark of the truth" is *the Church* (1 Tim 3:15).

CHAPTER 7

Stoic Strivings: The Slave, the Lawyer, the Emperor, and God

"Philosophy's power to blunt all the blows of circumstance is beyond belief. Never a single missile lodges in her; she has strong, impenetrable defenses; some blows she breaks the force of, parrying them with the slack of her gown as if they were trivial, others she flings off and hurls back at the sender."

SENECA, *Letter 53*[1]

"How can a man find a sensible way to live? One way and one only — philosophy. And my philosophy means keeping that vital spark within you free from damage and degradation, using it to transcend pain and pleasure, doing everything with a purpose, avoiding lies and hypocrisy, not relying on another person's actions or failings. To accept everything that comes, and everything that is given, as coming from that same spiritual source."

MARCUS AURELIUS, *Meditations* (II,17)[2]

"What else can I, a lame old man, do but sing hymns to God? If, indeed, I were a nightingale, I should be singing as a nightingale; if a swan, as a swan. But as it is, I am a rational being, therefore I must be singing hymns of praise to God. This is my task; I do it, and will not desert this post, as long as it may be given me to fill it; and I exhort you to join me in this same song."

EPICTETUS, *Discourses* (Book 1.16)[3]

I've always admired the ancient Greeks and Romans, probably as much as I did Superman — and undoubtedly, at first, because of Superman's ancient Greek ancestor, Herakles (or Hercules, in the more familiar Latin). Somewhere early on, I must have heard the story or seen a movie or cartoon showing Hercules kneeling down, intertwining his fingers, and slamming his fists on the ground, producing a nice little earthquake, the kind where the ground is visibly rent asunder, cleaved in twain, or just plain split in two, if you prefer. I tried this with most focused attention several times as a young child. I didn't have much luck.

A few years later, I ordered these weighted "Hercules wristbands" from the back of a comic book. They were guaranteed to make your arms bulge — and to make you unbeatable in arm wrestling. Still, Hercules wristbands and all, I could not get the earth to budge. I never gave up on those ancient Greeks and Romans, though. But later my interest shifted from the myths of their strong men to the truths of their wise men, and it was the writings of Chapter 3's Albert Ellis that first led me to three of their wisest.

Three Wise Men From the West

Stoicism was a school of ancient philosophy founded by Zeno of Citium (c. 335-c. 263 B.C.). The name of their school simply derives from a particular covered porch (*stoa* in Greek), from which Zeno taught in Athens, being unable to afford a building. Zeno was most strongly influenced by the philosopher Socrates, who so fervently sought truth, and by the Cynic philosophers, who taught that the good life was a life of virtue, and that other things, like worldly goods and sensual pleasures, were not true goods worth pursuing. Only fragments of Zeno's writings survived, but we are very fortunate to have substantial written records from three of the most prominent, profound, and practical of his philosophical progeny. These are the lawyer, the emperor, and the slave of our chapter title.

Seneca: Silver-Tongued Stoic Stylist

Lucius Annaeus Seneca (4 B.C.-A.D. 65) was born in Spain, but attained great success in Rome as an attorney, politician, literary figure, amateur scientist, and philosopher. Seneca acquired tremendous influence, being the adviser to a young Nero, who, after shunning Seneca's counsel, achieved infamy as persecutor of the Christians and scourge to Rome itself.

Seneca was very well-versed in Stoic philosophy. A refined and brilliant gentleman, he expressed profound thoughts with clarity, and with panache. Although he was also a man of extreme wealth and vast land holdings, he preached a life of simplicity. When criticized that he did not always practice what he preached — for example, by retaining his great wealth — he said he did not claim to be a philosophical sage himself, but a student and seeker of wisdom like the rest of us.

Seneca was a prolific writer, and we still have many volumes of his philosophical works. He wrote complete treatises on many topics, including those on anger, on consoling people who have lost loved ones, on the happy life, and on benefits and gratitude. He also wrote 124 letters to a friend named Lucilius, with the obvious intention that they be widely read for millennia to come.

In these letters and essays, Seneca masterfully counsels us on issues of simplicity and satisfaction: "It is not the man who has too little who is poor, but the one who hankers after more."[4] On artfully influencing the unphilosophical for their own good: "Let our aim be a way of life not diametrically opposed to, but better than that of the mob. Otherwise we shall repel and alienate the very people whose reform we desire."[5] On fellowship: "The first thing philosophy promises us is the feeling of fellowship, of belonging to mankind and being members of a community."[6] On learning and sharing: "Part of my joy in learning is that it puts me in a position to teach[7] ... there is no enjoying the possession of anything unless one has someone to share it with."[8] And there is so much more.

Seneca, like all three of the wise men we'll meet, loved philosophy, not as some abstract network of ideas, but as a real and practical guide to the good life. Refer, if you will to his quotation at the start of the chapter. There is Lady Philosophy, invincible, deflecting and hurling back potential attacks, just like Superman did in Chapter 3 (which I wrote before I came across this quotation again). Seneca was also all for the positive influence of heroes: "We need to set our affections on some good man and keep him constantly before our eyes, so that we may live as if he were watching us, and do everything as if he saw what we were doing."[9]

I had come across bits and pieces of the writings of Seneca in my youth, but he had the most profound effect on me in my early 40s. Having gone through a doctoral program while working full-time, teaching on the side, and raising young boys with my wife, it was after reading one of his pithy quotes in the spring of 2004 that I decided I would work on the side as a professor no more. That decision, in turn, led to the chain of events that year that brought me back to Christ and His Church. The quote was this: *"Nihil minus est hominis occupati quam vivere"* ("There is nothing the busy man is less busied with than living").[10] And of course, by this he means the man who is *too* busy, the one who has scheduled his life in such a way that he has left little time for leisure and reflection. Socrates, a hero to the Stoics, put it this way: "The unexamined life is not worth living."

We'll come back to Seneca in our last section of this chapter, and we'll see him again in the chapter on St. Thomas

Aquinas. For now, let's briefly examine the life of the next wise man of the West, who was indeed a king — in fact, a Roman emperor.

Marcus Aurelius: Meditations of a Philosopher-King

Marcus Aurelius Antoninus Augustus (A.D. 121-180) was emperor of the Roman Empire for the last 19 years of his life. When historian Edward Gibbon wrote his famous *Decline and Fall of the Roman Empire*, he declared the reign of Marcus Aurelius the most glorious and happy peak that preceded that decline. Marcus Aurelius is also known today as the author of one book, what we now simply call *Meditations*, a timeless classic that may have never been intended for publication.

Marcus was by temperament a man of deep thought, generosity, and gratitude. As a youth, when required to attend gladiatorial battles at the Colosseum or chariot races at the Circus Maximus, he would bring along a good book to read. In middle age, and until his death, this man of ideas, this benevolent professor by nature, found himself year after year on the frozen banks of German rivers commanding the legions of Rome in defense of the world's greatest empire. But in the evenings, this reluctant man of war sheathed his sword and drew forth his pen, which has truly had mightier and farther-reaching results. At day's end, he became a philosopher, to console his spirit, to cajole himself to virtue, and whether he intended to or not, to provide similar consolation and inspiration to pagans and Christians alike for nearly two millennia.

A self-described pagan co-worker told me she keeps the *Meditations* near her nightstand. P. G. Wodehouse's fictional genius and gentleman's gentleman Jeeves is most fond of quoting Marcus Aurelius. Recently, while reading the diaries of Elisabeth Leseur — pages so poignant and powerful that after her death, her atheistic husband was led to the Church and to the priesthood — I came across some lines that made me think, "Hey, she knew the Stoics!" On the very next page, there was the name of Marcus Aurelius.

So what exactly did this emperor write? I'll supply but a few enticing snippets.

The first chapter of the *Meditations* consists of Marcus's catalog of thanks to various family members and teachers who influenced him, including one Sextus, grandson of the philosopher Plutarch, from whom he learned "kindliness... and dignity without affectation; and an intuitive consideration for friends; and a toleration for the unlearned and the unreasoning. And his tactful treatment of all his friends, so that simply to be with him was more delightful than any flattery...."[11] From Alexander the Grammarian, Marcus learned not to embarrass others by correcting their speech, but if possible, to later employ the correct pronunciation or usage in a statement of one's own, to subtly provide the proper example. This future emperor also learned "a readiness to acknowledge without jealousy the claims of those who were endowed with any special gift, such as eloquence or knowledge of the law or ethics of any other subject...."[12]

Specific virtues Marcus acknowledges in various mentors include "sweetness of temper,"[13] modesty, manliness, generosity, abstention, simplicity, self-reliance, control of anger, "to possess great learning but make no parade of it";[14] love of family, truth, and justice; optimism, confidence, stability, self-mastery, cheeriness, beneficence, mildness, unshakable steadfastness, love of work and the common good, sexual self-restraint, good humor, and foresightedness. That's quite a list for just his first chapter. But how do we acquire these things? Let's meditate for a moment on his very first meditation to find out.

In Book II of the *Meditations*, Marcus Aurelius begins with a paragraph of advice that we might all do well to read first thing every day, right after morning prayers. The kindly emperor tells us that upon arising each day, we should say to ourselves that we are going to encounter "the busybody, the thankless, the overbearing, the treacherous, the envious, the unneighborly"[15] — and though more than 668,000 days have passed since he wrote those words, I think they still ring true for us today. He goes on to say that we should remind ourselves that they act this way because they do not truly understand the beauty of goodness and the ugliness of evil; that we cannot truly be debased or injured by them if we *do* understand the good; that they share with us the same humanity and capacity for reason; and that we cannot hate them, but must value them as kinsmen, placed in the world for cooperation, and not for resentment and aversion. Whew!

In other words, Marcus tells us that we can remain calm in our minds and loving in our hearts if we forgive one another's faults — in advance! If I may call to mind Dr. Ellis's ABC scheme (see page 61) — inspired by the Stoics after all — the emperor would have us plant rational beliefs in our mind ahead of time, ready to spring forth to counter life's little unfortunate events that are simply bound to happen.

We have only reviewed a few of the hundreds of the emperor's thoughts. But it is now time to move on to the slave who taught the emperor.

Epictetus: Zeus's Lame Messenger

Marcus Aurelius thanked a man named Rusticus for making him acquainted with the *Memoirs of Epictetus*, and now we turn to the man behind the memoirs. Epictetus (c. A.D. 55-c. 135) was a freed slave of Phrygia who, like Seneca, lived in Rome during Nero's reign. He was banished from Rome, along with all of the philosophers, by Emperor Domitian around the year 90, and taught for the rest of his life in the Greek city of Nicopolis. We have no surviving writings of Epictetus himself, but his student Arrian wrote down his lectures, leaving us two main compilations of Epictetus's philosophy. The first, called the *Enchiridion* (handbook) — in 53 chapters, with each chapter usually consisting of one paragraph to a page — is a brief summary or distillation of the main principles of Epictetus's thought. Relatively dry and straightforward, its profound lessons have influenced millions for centuries. It is in the *Discourses,* purportedly near-verbatim transcripts of Epictetus's lectures, that we see the self-proclaimed lame old man come alive — sometimes blunt, sometimes gruff, but always sincere and profound. And so, what are his primary lessons?

We read in the *Enchiridion* that "it is not things themselves that disturb men, but their judgements about these things."[16] So, let things be "A," disturbances be "C," and judgments be "B." There you have Ellis's ABC theory of emotion and the cornerstone of all modern cognitive psychotherapies — this line from Epictetus is their acknowledged source! The first sentence of the *Enchiridion* tells us, "Some things are under our control, while others are not under our control,"[17] and that the wise man will waste no time giving inordinate care to things he cannot control — including our property, our physical health, and the behavior of other people toward us. The primary thing under our control is our own view of things and our own "moral purpose."

True freedom and true wisdom consist in controlling our own thinking and desiring. So, then, let's listen as Epictetus asks himself what a Stoic Superman would look like:

> Who, then, is the invincible man? He whom nothing that is outside the sphere of his moral purpose can dismay.[18]

Epictetus believed that man was created in the image of God, in terms of the ability to reason and to choose, and that man's highest purpose was to merge his will with God's will by full exercise of that reason, honed through the pursuit of philosophy — *philos* + *sophia*, from the Greek, meaning, literally, "the love of wisdom." This endeavor is consonant with the building of virtue and self-control, in training oneself to desire and act for only what is good and right.

There are countless worthwhile corollary ideas and maxims. One is that beginners in philosophy blame others when things go wrong; those starting to learn blame themselves; and the truly wise blame nobody, but focus on setting things aright. Epictetus advises detachment from material goods, considering them as "indifferents." He tells of the time that a brass lamp, one of his few possessions, was stolen. He simply replaced it with a clay one, while he questioned the wisdom of the thief who would sell his own moral purpose for the price of a simple brass lamp. When told that someone had talked about one of his faults, his response (to paraphrase) was: "Surely they did not know about all of my others, or they would have brought those up, too."

Epictetus's ultimate man was no evolutionary superman, but the wise philosopher-sage who had built his virtue and self-control to a level of inward invincibility. But what was the true foundation of that invincibility? I didn't see it when I saw the Stoics through the glasses of Albert Ellis, but I did when I saw their own writings directly through my own contact lenses. And this is what I saw.

The Porch and the Cross

There is quite an interesting history of the intersecting courses of Stoic philosophy and Christian theology. Seneca's own elder brother, the governor Gallio, is quoted within the pages of the New Testament itself (Acts 18: 14-15), where he refuses to hear a case against St. Paul. There was once even a book claiming to have correspondence between Seneca himself and St. Paul, but it was found to be unauthentic. Epictetus made only a few passing comments about Christians in his writings (recall that he died long before the Bible had been assembled), but lessons from his *Enchiridion* were incorporated into some ancient monastic rules. Although Marcus Aurelius's reign was marked by some persecution of Christians, it is unlikely that he himself instigated it — but his failure to stop it does point to the limitations of the Stoic philosophy.

In the Middle Ages, Scholastic schoolmen were well aware of Seneca, who wrote in Latin, and we will see that St. Thomas Aquinas would cite him in many places within the *Summa Theologica*.

The Stoics also had a very influential role regarding my own personal journey back to Christianity. Since my early 20s, I had been a big fan of Ellis's Rational Emotive Behavior Therapy because I knew it worked. I also respected the Stoics because I knew they were its main precursors. There was no doubt in my mind that these three ancient sages knew far more of value about the human mind, emotion, and behavior than any gaggle of modern behaviorist or psychoanalytic psychologists.

Oddly enough, though, while Ellis was an avowed atheist, Seneca, Marcus Aurelius, and Epictetus were believers, one and all. (I figured at the time that nobody's perfect.) Though we tend to think of the ancient Greeks and Romans in terms of their classic polytheistic pantheon of Olympian gods, the Stoics were much more likely to speak of God with a Capital "G." They did not know Christ, but their reason led them to belief in one God, which they sometimes referred to as Zeus, or Nature, or Providence. Epictetus, in particular, though, spoke of God in personal terms. Recall this "lame old man's" hymns to God at the start of this chapter. And here's an anonymous epigram found in the writings of St. John Chrysostom: "Slave, poor as Irus, halting as I trod, I, Epictetus, was the friend of God."[19] It was when I had obtained that leisure which Seneca advised that I found myself freer to focus on my own moral purpose à la Epictetus — and before long, to say of all things and events around me, like Marcus Aurelius, "This has come from God."

Actually, though, I profited greatly from *two* groups of ancient Greek wise men bearing gifts: not only the Stoics, but also the Aristotelians. In the next chapter, we'll turn to a modern Aristotelian, a contemporary of Albert Ellis, who had actually once debated Bertrand Russell. It was in revisiting his thoughts in my early 40s that I was soon drawn back to Aristotle, then over to St. Thomas Aquinas, and all the way up to Christ, the same path that this Aristotelian had taken in his 90-plus years of life.

TRUTH BOX #7

Divine Ideas

God is one and the same with Reason, Fate, and Zeus.

The Stoics were no atheists. Though there were, of course, no new Darwinian atheists at the time of their philosophical heyday, there were indeed materialistic atheists of other schools, such as the Atomists, most notably Democritus and Leucippus, who saw all of reality as composed of atoms moving about according to chance, leaving no room for the soul or for spiritual beings. Other philosophers, like the Epicureans, most notably Epicurus himself and Lucretius, drew from the Atomists; and, while still believing in gods, paved the way for further atheism by arguing that the gods were uninterested and unable to intervene in our affairs. They also denied an afterlife.

The Stoics did not deny the spiritual realm, and they saw the reality of a single God. Aided by reason but lacking in divine revelation, they had varied conceptions of God that captured pieces and parts of the truths of His nature.

God was considered a spiritual and active principle that gives shape and meaning to a primary passive principle of undifferentiated matter. The ancient Greeks, you see, had a conception of an eternal universe ("existence exists") and perceived God as a First Cause in terms of changing matter, rather than bringing the universe into existence *ex nihilo* — that is, out of nothing. The Stoics had rather vague and sometimes conflicting understandings of God as the shaper of the cosmos, or universe; as the "soul" of the universe; or as the universe itself. Some held, therefore, a rather pantheistic view that everything is God, or a part of God. Some saw Him as synonymous with Nature or with Fate. Others, at times, especially Epictetus, did see God as a personal, father-like figure interested in our existence.

Regardless of their rather murky concepts of God, the Stoics acknowledged Him based on reason alone. They also deduced from His existence our need to live lives of virtue and self-control, and they developed very effective techniques to help us achieve this. There is still much that good Christians can learn from those teachers on the porch.

CHAPTER 8

Mortimer Adler and the God of the Philosophers

"In the case of contradictories, no middle ground is possible. The theistic affirmation God exists *and the atheistic denial* God does not exist *stand in contradiction to one another; both cannot be true and both cannot be false; if one is true, the other must be false."*

MORTIMER ADLER, Truth in Religion[1]

"Philosophical theology may carry one's mind to the edge of religious belief, but that is the near edge of a chasm that can only be crossed to the far edge by a leap of faith that transcends reason."

MORTIMER ADLER, Truth in Religion[2]

"When persons of religious faith say that 'God is love,' or, perhaps more accurately, that 'God loves,' they do so by virtue of their believing in the supreme being as the creator and preserver of the cosmos. To make something and to preserve it is an act of love, a benevolent overflowing of the maker's being into the being of something else."

MORTIMER ADLER, How to Think About God[3]

Sometimes the most profound ideas are the simplest. They appeal to our common sense. Have you ever read a presentation of some abstract theory and thought: *Oh yes, that makes perfect sense. Why didn't I think of that?* On the other hand, have you ever read some presentation of an abstract theory and thought: *Oh no, what on earth is the author even saying? How could he possibly think that makes sense, or that anyone would understand him?* There is a fair amount of writing out there today of the "Oh no" variety.

In 1996, physicist Alan Sokal published an article entitled "Transgressing the Boundaries: Toward a Transformative Hermeneutics of Quantum Gravity" in the journal *Social Text*. Perhaps that title generated a "What on earth is the author even saying?" response in you. Well, it apparently did not to the editors of the avant-garde, "postmodernist" journal in which it was published.

You see, in 1998, the article's creator produced the book *Fashionable Nonsense: Postmodern Intellectuals' Abuse of Science*,[4] in which he, and the book's co-author, Jean Bricmont, revealed that Sokal's article was indeed a hoax, fabricated gobbledygook that made no sense — and the journal's own editorial staff was *not* in on the joke! Sadly, such lack of clarity, meaning, and truth seems to make little difference in some academic circles these days. Sokal wrote the article as a protest against some contemporary humanist writers who played loosely with theories in math and science (not to mention with language), and whose writings, in effect, argued against objective truth, common sense, and reason.

Moritmer Adler (1902-2001) was no postmodernist, or even a modernist, for that matter. He was no fan of fashion, or of nonsense. He championed great books and great ideas, eternal truths and man's capacity for grasping them. It was Adler who introduced me to the powerful logic and common sense appeal of that ancient enemy of nonsense, Aristotle, the Father of Logic, through his book *Aristotle for Everybody: Difficult Thought Made Easy*.[5] Adler had little tolerance for academic jargon, and he strove to share the fruits of philosophy with everybody, as did the Stoics and Aristotelians of old. Philosophy, for Adler, was a means to actually improve the lives of the man and woman on the street. He wrote his books for you and me.

Adler tells the tale of the time when, as a young man, he had the daunting task of debating the older and celebrated Bertrand Russell on an educational topic. He said that after laying out a fully prepared and logically structured outline of his points, Russell took the podium with nary a note and scarcely a thought about the topic beforehand, complimented Adler on his "rugged simplicity," and went on quipping away, wowing the audience more perhaps with his wit, than with his wisdom. Adler, you see, could be a little dry at times, but thorough, clear, logical, and, yes, "ruggedly simple." Unfortunately, though, modern audiences often crave the clever and crafty sound bite over the ruggedly simple truth.

Adler was one of the earliest and greatest proponents of the "great books" curricula at the university level, where students would study, not secondhand textbooks, but the actual writings of the greatest thinkers in human history, from Aristotle to Aquinas, from Homer to Shakespeare, and so many more in philosophy, literature, history, mathematics, science, and religion. Adler drew fame early on with his bestselling book *How to Read a Book* (1940)[6] — suffering, no doubt, through countless inquiries of how one was supposed to read it unless he already knew how in the first place! As the subtitle, *The Art of Getting a Liberal Education*, suggests, it was actually about how to read books more effectively, of course.

(One of his many recommendations, by the way, was to mark them up and write in the margins, encouraging reflection and making the book one's own. So please know that I won't mind if you get out your pencil and go to town right here on these pages, even if to take me to task now and then — unless this happens to be a library loaner copy!)

I admired Adler a great deal in my youth for his connection with the old-fashioned ideas of the importance of acquiring a broad knowledge base, of developing the habits of thinking clearly and logically, of respecting the achievements of the greatest minds of humanity, and of the value of philosophical thinking in improving human life.

The 20th-Century Jewish-Pagan-Thomist

The Catholic Church teaches us that reason can lead us to the existence of God. St. Paul tells us as much: "Ever since the creation of the world his invisible nature, namely, his eternal power and deity, has been clearly perceived in the things that have been made" (Rom 1:20). Well, I went through Catholic grade school, Catholic high school, and one year of Catholic college, and either this point was not clearly presented to me or I wasn't paying attention. By the time I first found Mortimer Adler's writings in my early 20s, I had abandoned a belief in God, but by no means had I abandoned a belief in logic, truth, or the unique powers of the human mind. So I gobbled up several of Adler's books, on things like the great ideas and the human intellect.

After a few years immersed in atheism, though, I recall reading one book with an unusual interest and with some measure of hope: *How to Think About God*. You see, I recall thinking at the time that I would be quite pleased if Adler could convince me to reject atheism and embrace God once more. He proceeded through several classical proofs of God's existence in that book, showing what he saw as the fatal chinks in their armor; but he concluded with his own proof, a slight variation on one of the classics, that he found to be invulnerable.

Adler's subtitle for that book was *A Guide for the 20th-Century Pagan*, and he defined the 20th-century pagan as the person who had grown up immersed in the culture shaped by the great Western monotheistic religions — Christianity, Judaism, and Islam — whose mind was shaped by modern science, and who did not believe in God. At the time he produced that book (1980) he was one, and so was I. Borrowing from the French scientist Blaise Pascal, Adler went on to define two different classes of pagans, derived from three classes of mankind, namely:

1. "Those who know God and love him."
2. "Those who do not know God but seek him."
3. "Those who neither know God nor seek him."[7]

Groups 2 and 3 referred, of course, to the pagans. Adler, though raised in a nominally Jewish household, would spend most of his adult career in the second of those classes. When I first read this book, in my 20s, I had spent several years by then in Group 3, thinking there really was no God to seek. But maybe I was actually about a 2.5, since I was intrigued by the book and wondered if it could at least get me actually seeking again. It was to be a *second* reading of this book, almost 20 years later, that was one of the things that helped move me from the Group 2 spot all the way back to Group 1.

I'll soon provide, in the most compact of nutshells, Adler's argument. But first, let me give you a little background on Dr. Adler's unusual philosophical and theological stance.

You see, our 20th-century Jewish pagan was also… a Thomist! He had been greatly intrigued and influenced throughout his career by the writings of St. Thomas Aquinas, the greatest theological doctor of the Catholic Church. So, in his book on thinking about God, he addresses several classical proofs, or demonstrations, of God's existence, from great doctors like St. Anselm and St. Thomas Aquinas, and then he provides a variation of his own.

The God of the Philosophers

Now let's remember from the start that Adler is working here purely within the realm of reason, with no room for faith or divine revelation. *How to Think About God* is an exercise in reason alone. That said, Adler begins by stating that the universe or cosmos must either have *existed eternally* (recall the Greeks, Rand and the Objectivists, and "existence exists") *or have been created*. He notes that if we assume from the start that the universe was created, then, of course, there must be a Creator. He therefore tries to build his proof of God's existence on the assumption that the universe itself is also eternal.

Adler believed that some findings in modern physics challenged some older proofs. For example, he believed that the modern understanding of *inertia* — noting that not only resting bodies will continue to rest, but that bodies in motion will continue to move unless acted upon by another force — called into question arguments necessitating God's continuing action in the world. He noted that the concept of the *conservation of matter* raised questions about God's role in keeping individual things in existence, since matter seems only to change, but never ceases to exist. The classical argument, he pointed out, had been that individual beings have *contingent* being — they either might or might not exist, or continue to exist — while only God has *necessary* being, and simply must exist.

What follows is the gist of the argument that Adler found to be true — if not certainly true, then at least "beyond a reasonable doubt." Though "ruggedly simple," the argument contains its complexities, so if it intrigues you, please check out Adler's own full rendering as well.

Although nothing within the material universe is actually *annihilated* — goes completely out of existence — neither is any individual thing within the material universe *exnihilated* — brought into being out of nothing. It is not within the power of nature and matter to produce something from nothing. But what about the entire universe, or cosmos, itself? If the whole cosmos could have been different, if other universes with different natural laws and ordered arrangements could have been or could yet be possible in the infinite past or future, then *all of the material existence as we know it is itself contingent.* We know that "existence exists," but it is also possible that it could *cease* to exist. "A cosmos which can *be otherwise* is one that also can *not be....*"[8]

Now, we know that nothing within the natural order of the material universe is annihilated or exnihilated. This requires something above and beyond *matter* and *nature,* something *spiritual* and *supernatural.* This, then, is the God that Adler argues can be shown as necessary for *preserving* the universe in its existence, *even if we start our chain of reasoning with the assumption that the universe has always existed.* He then writes that once we have proven God's necessity under that assumption, "we can turn to the more likely assumption of a created cosmos,"[9] of God not only as the *Preserver* of the universe, but as its *Creator.*

The God of Abraham, Isaac, and Jacob

Adler argues that belief in God as the Creator of the universe, what Pascal called "the God of the philosophers," *does not* require a leap of faith. But what about the God of the Bible? Belief in the triune God of Christianity *does* require a leap of faith, but Adler argues that reason can also help bridge the chasm. Based on what we can infer from God's capacity to create the universe *ex nihilo* (from nothing), we can conclude that He is a supreme, omnipotent, immaterial, living, all-knowing, and willing being. We can deduce that God has "*aseity*" — which is "to have existence from, through, and in one's self."[10]

Recall, if you will, that God gave His name to Moses as *Yahweh*: "I AM WHO I AM" (Ex 3:14). Further, He said: "Say this to the sons of Israel, 'I AM has sent me to you... the God of your fathers, the God of Abraham, the God of Isaac, and the God of Jacob...' " (Ex 3:14, 15). Adler also notes that by rational examination of human nature, we can conclude that man has a special status in all of nature by virtue of his intellectual powers, making him the only creature that is more than a thing: a *person*. This is quite consistent with the idea of man as a creature made in God's image. (Adler wrote a book on this subject called *The Difference of Man and the Difference It Makes*.[11] It was one of the books that led me back to Christ, and I'll tell that story in the next chapter.)

Also, from the fact that the preserver and creator of the universe is self-sufficient, and yet chooses to create and sustain the entirety of the cosmos, it is entirely consistent to conclude that He is all-loving, as well as all-powerful and all-knowing. There is also reason to believe that He has the capacity, the knowledge, and the will to know and care for each one of us personally. The concept of a personal, loving God, then, is no affront to reason.

How the Pagan Eagle Flew to the Church

Adler concluded *How to Think About God* with a section entitled "Adverse Views," in which he cited books and articles by philosophers who disagreed with his thesis that reason leads to God. One was a book entitled *God and Philosophy*, by distinguished British philosopher Antony Flew. That book, published in 1966, was one of Flew's many scholarly tomes propounding that reason leads to atheism. Perhaps, though, you've come across a book Professor Flew wrote 42 years later, happily entitled *There Is a God: How the World's Most Notorious Atheist Changed His Mind*.[12] Through his continued philosophical ponderings and musings on modern science, one of the world's foremost philosophers and atheists is no longer in the "adverse views" camp.

Why did Flew reverse his long-held positions? Noting that he, like Socrates before him, always said that he must go wherever the arguments led him, he found himself led to God. And he found God the Creator to be reasonable. Flew also acknowledged that the God of Aristotle — unchanging, immaterial, omnipotent, omniscient, one, indivisible, perfectly good, and necessarily existing (the God of the philosophers) — is also quite consistent with God as described within the Judeo-Christian tradition (the God of Abraham, Isaac, and Jacob). He wrote that he had no personal religious experience or revelation. "In short, my discovery of the Divine has been a pilgrimage of reason and not faith."[13] Yet even so, in a section labeled "Open to Learning More," he would comment that "no other religion enjoys anything like the combination of a charismatic figure like Jesus and a first-class intellectual like St. Paul. If you want omnipotence to set up a religion, it seems to me that this [Christianity] is the one to beat!"[14]

Two questions remain to be answered in this chapter. (1) Did Mortimer Adler change *his* views in the last two decades of his life? (Surely, he and Antony Flew didn't swap their positions, did they?) And (2) what do "pagan eagles" have to do with all of this? I'm going to answer the second question first.

The "pagan eagle" refers to Adler himself because (a) he called himself a pagan when he wrote *How to Think About God*, (b) "*adler*" is the German word for eagle, and (c) because it also allowed for a quirky heading fitting in Flew's name. Now, on to more serious business.

We saw with Professor Flew that the atheist became a theist. As for the "pagan," I knew before I started writing this book that Mortimer Adler had indeed taken the leap across the chasm and become a Christian — an Episcopalian, to be precise — in April 1984. What I was delighted, though not completely surprised, to find out only recently is that two years before his death, at the age of 96, this Jewish-pagan-Thomist came home to the Church of St. Thomas, St. Peter, and Christ. In December 1999, Dr. Adler, the *ex*-pagan, became a Roman Catholic.

TRUTH BOX #8

You Call This Progress?

1. *Philosophy has progressed and advanced since the days of Aristotle.*
2. *Philosophy has not progressed and advanced since the days of Aristotle.*

Some proponents of modern philosophy, and definitely those of the "postmodernist" persuasion who deny objective truth, will argue that the basic fundamental laws of philosophical reasoning and definition of terms laid down by Aristotle are passé, and have been superseded — all of which ignores the fact that they must make use of objective rules of logic and clearly defined meanings if they are to propose any kind of rational argument at all. Indeed, once, about 10 years ago, a letter to the editor of *Mensa Bulletin* described the thought of Aristotle as a mere "historical curiosity." I wrote in response that I prayed that we should all then become more "historically curious!"

Other moderns and postmoderns with little taste for philosophy will argue that philosophy has *not* progressed at all since its classical heyday with the ancients, having arrived at its stagnant dead-end millennia ago. This is not quite true either. Aristotle made explicit some very fundamental laws of human reasoning — things like the law, or axiom, of non-contradiction and the concepts of causality, which remain the *philosophia perennis*, true for all time, because they represent fundamental and unchanging truths.

Aristotle, of course, was not infallible. There are many factual errors in his writings (albeit there are those who believe that some of his works are actually the surviving lecture notes of his students). But when he is found in error, we can use his own stated principles of reasoning to show it.

The most profound perfection of Aristotle's philosophy is found in the work of the modern Thomists — and in the next chapter, we'll take a look at "Thom" himself.

PART III

Christ Has Risen From His Tomb!

"The human intellect, to which it is connatural to derive its knowledge from sensible things, is not able through itself to reach the vision of the divine substance in itself, which is above all sensible things.... Yet... man may progress in the knowledge of God by beginning with lower things and gradually ascending....

So that man might have a firmer knowledge of Him, God revealed certain things about Himself that transcend the human intellect....

Thus, then, are we taught from Sacred Scripture that the Son of God, begotten of God, is God.

ST. THOMAS AQUINAS, *Summa Contra Gentiles*
(Book 4, 1,1; 1:3; 3:3)[1]

CHAPTER 9

St. Thomas Aquinas:
The Angelic Doctor Effects a Cure

"There are many who, with minds alienated from the Faith, hate all Catholic teaching, and say that reason alone is their teacher and guide. To heal these men of their unbelief, and to bring them to grace and the Catholic Faith, we think that nothing[,] after the supernatural help of God, can be more useful in these days than the solid doctrine of the Fathers and the Scholastics."

POPE LEO XIII, *Aeterni Patris*[1]

"Accordingly, as is was said to the Egyptians of old in time of famine, 'Go to Joseph,' so that they should receive a supply of corn from him to nourish their bodies, so we now say to all such as are desirous of the truth, 'Go to Thomas,' and ask him to give you from his ample store the food of substantial doctrine wherewith to nourish your souls unto eternal life."

POPE PIUS XI, *Studiorum Ducem*[2]

"The Church has been justified in consistently proposing St. Thomas as a master of thought and a model of the right way to do theology."

POPE JOHN PAUL II, *Fides et Ratio*[3]

As pure as his intentions, and as glorious as his powers may be, everyone knows that the comic book Man of Steel is not completely invincible. Superman has his kryptonite, as Achilles had his heel, and Samson had his hair. The story of virtually every great hero includes some element of his weakness and vulnerability as well. What some modern atheists seem to forget is that we are men and not gods, let alone God. Our powers, though great, are not limitless and infallible, and this includes our powers of reason, and even of the scientific method.

For more than 20 years, I was rather confident in my powers of reasoning that led me to atheism. Certainly, I was no open enemy of God. I actually wished that I could believe, but in all honesty, I could not. Though I rarely darkened the door of a church, my wife, Kathy (a Catholic convert), and I did send our sons to Catholic schools. I knew that I had obtained something very good from my own experience there, not just in terms of academics, but in terms of building upon a fundamental sense of right and wrong, and a desire to do good.

It is a popular cliché today to speak of "Catholic guilt" as a remnant of old-fashioned childhood indoctrination that enlightened folks would be wise to cast off. I, on the other hand, even while an atheist, considered that guilt as a sign of a formed conscience that knows right from wrong, compelling one to set things right when wrong has been done. Some warn, too, along with Dostoyevsky and others, that without God, anything goes, and that there is no need or reason to be moral. I never thought that myself. I was too steeped in the classical virtues to ever accept modern relativistic ideas that deny the existence of right and wrong. So, then, even while outside the Church, I knew quite well that there was much good within it. I felt, however, that while the Church was right about many things regarding moral behaviors and the dignity of man — things like the value of honesty, courage, self-control, and loving kindness — it was wrong in its most fundamental premise and promise: that there is a God who created man and who lies at the heart of this moral order.

How did I end up leaving the Church in 1980, and what brought me back in 2004? Pope Leo XIII had the answer in 1879. I refer you to the quotation from his encyclical *Aeterni Patris* (on the restoration of Christian philosophy according to the mind of St. Thomas Aquinas, the Angelic Doctor) that begins this chapter. I was one who had come to believe that reason alone was my guide, and it was through the grace of God that decades later I was led to the writings of the greatest of the Catholic Scholastics, St. Thomas Aquinas — and that's what brought me home to Athens, Jerusalem, and Rome.

So how did a thoughtful and bookish young man immersed in a Catholic grade school and high school not know about those Scholastics and Church Fathers in the first place? Good question. Indeed, I spent my first nine years of schooling under the tutelage of fine Dominican sisters, the order of St. Thomas himself. Thomas is the patron saint of Catholic schools to boot. Was I not paying attention, or was I not being taught about the great intellectual heritage of our own Church?

Of course, I went through Catholic schools (from 1966 to 1979) during those rather tumultuous years of American cultural upheaval coinciding with those first post-Vatican II years, as interpretations and misinterpretations of the Church's goals and visions ran rampant. I believe it was a time when much of our glorious heritage was downplayed or ignored, with tragic results. Indeed, in the words of Pope John Paul II himself:

In the years after the Second Vatican Council, many Catholic faculties were in some ways impoverished by a diminished sense of the importance of the study not just of Scholastic philosophy but more generally of the study of philosophy itself. I cannot fail to note with surprise and displeasure that this lack of interest in the study of philosophy is shared by not a few theologians.[4]

In thinking back on my years of religion classes, I recall gaining some familiarity with some classic biblical stories, though probably less than what many of my Protestant peers obtained in their Sunday schools. (A song about Jesus and Zacchaeus is one tidbit that sticks in my mind.) As for the great Church Fathers and Scholastics — Sts. Augustine, Jerome, Clement of Rome and Clement of Alexandria, Irenaeus, Gregory the Great, Albert the Great, Thomas Aquinas, and so many others — my knowledge was virtually nonexistent. Surely, the names of at least St. Augustine and St. Thomas had come up at some time, but I truly don't recall it.

In seventh grade, one of our parish priests came in to answer our questions on religion. He fielded questions like whether God could create a boulder so heavy even He couldn't lift it, and other whoppers of that sort. Decades later, I realized that he was probably using his knowledge of St. Thomas's theological and philosophical writings when he answered such doozies, but I don't recall any mention of Aquinas at that time or at any other time, until I took a philosophy course at a Catholic college.

Why would we not provide Catholic students with intellectual and spiritual heroes? I consider this unfortunate, especially since Pope Leo's encyclical from a hundred years earlier had been but one of many papal statements throughout the centuries encouraging that all Catholic teaching be founded upon the wisdom of St. Thomas.

The Patron Saint of Scholars in the Books of the Atheists (and at a State University)

My first recollections of St. Thomas Aquinas come from the writings of a couple of our atheists: Bertrand Russell, who tended to misrepresent and dismiss his approach, and Ayn Rand, who actually praised him. So why did Rand and the atheistic Objectivists praise St. Thomas? They rightly recognized that he brought the wisdom of Aristotle back to the Western world, elevating and expanding again the role of logic and reason in understanding the world and in guiding our lives. However, they also felt that his faith was his weakness, a point which I'll address later on.

I also chanced upon St. Thomas in one other very important place during my atheistic post-graduate years. In 1990, while preparing a master's thesis on the scientific research on using "mnemonic," or memory-improvement, techniques to bolster adolescents' academic performance, I chanced upon *The Art of Memory*, by Francis Yates. In this fascinating work, Yates detailed the history of "the art of memory," ancient techniques of memory improvement invented by the ancient Greeks and Romans. Interestingly, in the 13th century, these methods were perfected, adapted, and passed on to modern times by two of the most profound doctors of the Catholic Church, Sts. Albert the Great and Thomas Aquinas. Indeed, in the words of Yates herself: "If Simonides was the inventor of the art of memory, and 'Tulius' its teacher, Thomas Aquinas became something like its patron saint."[5]

The Porch, the Sun, and the Cross:
How I Came Back

I profited a lot from those Stoics we covered in Chapter 7. Please recall that these were originally the guys who taught under the porch. I wasn't totally with them, though, because I did not share their belief in God. Further, I had no idea that by spending too much time under their porch, I was blocking out the sun. You see, as I write now, I can look to the side of the room across from the Atlas globe and examine the statue of a man in a black and white robe, holding a book and a church. He wears the symbol of a large golden sun on his chest. To quote

Pope Leo XIII again, "he is likened to the sun; for he warmed the whole earth with the fire of his holiness, and filled the whole earth with the splendor of his teaching. There is no part of philosophy which he did not handle with acuteness and solidity."[6] He is St. Thomas Aquinas.

Because I so much loved a series of audio lectures on the Stoics I obtained around 2003, I bought additional courses on other philosophers and philosophies. One that I enjoyed on Aristotle was taught by Jesuit Father Joseph Koterski. Next, I purchased his DVD on natural law. (Both courses were produced by The Teaching Company.) In this latter course, I saw the Stoics, Aristotle, and St. Thomas Aquinas all as pivotal figures in understanding the nature of humanity, including our most fundamental political rights as human beings. How odd that all of them believed in God — and here again was that Catholic priest as the teacher. Hey, where were the atheistic champions of humanity? They played no major role in the theory of natural law. It was actually the recommended reading from this course that brought me back to the sun, the book, and the Church of St. Thomas Aquinas, and indeed to the cross of Jesus Christ. And I have since expressed my thanks to Father Koterski.

In examining the human nature that leads to human rights, one book on the recommended reading list was our own Dr. Mortimer Adler's *The Difference of Man and the Difference It Makes*. That insightful book prompted me to read again his *How to Think About God*. This, in turn, led me, at age 43, to read books specifically about and *by* St. Thomas Aquinas for the very first time in my life — and boy, was I in for a surprise!

It is reported that when Charles Darwin first read Aristotle's writings, he remarked that the scientific giants of the day were "mere schoolboys compared to old Aristotle." Well, when I first read St. Thomas Aquinas, I came to see that the likes of

Russell, Ellis, and Rand were indeed "mere schoolboys" (and a "schoolgirl") compared to old Aquinas!

How St. Thomas Lets the Sun (and Son) Shine In

Keeping with our illumination metaphor for St. Thomas Aquinas, there are many reasons this great saint shines so brilliantly. St. Thomas was gifted by God with an unusually powerful intellect and a prodigious memory. Exercising these personal qualities to the fullest, he focused his contemplation upon the highest and greatest of all possible objects: God. He was a profoundly humble man, and exceedingly docile (which means teachable — able to learn from others). Unlike many modern atheistic philosophers who assume that all deep thinking began with them, St. Thomas always looked for truth wherever it could be found and duly acknowledged those who had found it before him.

It was with no small amazement that I began to read his massive *Summa Theologica* for the very first time. Aquinas's mastery of the Scriptures is astounding, both in the vastness of his knowledge and in his subtlety of interpretation. He abounds in appropriate references to a huge variety of early Church Fathers, and even to Jewish and Muslim philosophers as well. Lo, had I only been aware of his utter mastery of the works of Aristotle and other ancients, including Cicero and Seneca, I would have become a full-blooded Thomist and been drawn back to Christ many years before.

St. Thomas's philosophy, like that of Ayn Rand's, was most strongly influenced by Aristotle's rational approach to the universe. Man is a creature with the desire and capacity to use his unique intellectual capacities to understand the world and guide his own actions. Rand's ethics, however, had only the loosest connections with Aristotle's. Indeed, I would come to wonder just how much she had really read of his works. There was absolutely no question in this regard with St. Thomas, however. He had written commentaries on Aristotle's books, including the *Nicomachean Ethics*, in which he had commented on every single line. Indeed, some argue that one can get a more complete understanding of Aristotle from St. Thomas than from Aristotle himself!

St. Thomas, of course, didn't just write as an Aristotelian philosopher. He also wrote as a Christian theologian. It was Aquinas who, like no one else before him or since, so completely displayed the harmony of human reasoning with Christian faith. Some thinkers in his day had argued that there were two truths, that one thing might be true in the realm of reason while the opposite might be true in the realm of faith. Some today may also believe that the truths of science and religion may likewise contradict one another. Wise St. Thomas would have nothing to do with this view. There is only one Truth, and though faith can take us to places that our power of reason cannot go, the truths of faith do not contradict the truths that we arrive at through the evidence of our senses and our reasoning powers.

The Creator, the Savior, the One, and the Three

It is said that from early childhood, St. Thomas's burning question was "What is God?" Recall that Bertrand Russell's pivotal question leading him away from faith was "Who made God?" Open the *Summa Theologica* or the *Summa Contra Gentiles* and you will see how the profundity of Aquinas's answers reveals the true childishness of Russell's very question, and a lack of ability to distinguish *the things made* from their *Maker*.

St. Thomas is famous for his "five ways" to logically demonstrate the existence of God, but I'm not going to address them at any length here. Though they have generated thousands of pages of commentary from myriads of commentators, he spends only one-and-a-half pages on them among the several thousand pages of the *Summa Theologica*!

You see, the entire body of Aquinas's writings attest to the existence and glorious supremacy of God. We can see this at a glance by looking at the structure of the *Summa Theologica*. This book of 38 treatises is divided into three main parts: God, Creation, and Christ. St. Thomas explains what we can learn about the true nature of God and of all creation (including ourselves) not only by pure reason, but also by the revelation that God has provided us through the divinely inspired Scriptures and through the actual physical incarnation (taking on of flesh by God the Son himself).

In using our reason, we learn about God as He is reflected indirectly in His creation. You and I, for example, are made in the image of God in terms of our capacities to understand and to guide our actions by our will. We understand through the reasoning powers of our intellectual soul, and we use our bodies as instruments to implement the choices of our will. God knows totally and immediately without any step-by-step reasoning process (being eternal, and not limited by temporal, sequential processes), and His will produces effects without any material instrument (hence His ability to create *ex nihilo* — from nothing).

We can deduce many things about God, including His eternity, His omnipotence, omniscience, and more. We can determine that God can do all things that are possible, non-contradictory, and consistent with truth. To ask if God could create a boulder so heavy that not even He could lift it is itself a contradictory question. Neither would God go back in time and make a previous event not happen, because to do so would turn a truth into a falsehood and bring about another contradiction.

Some atheists argue that the ideas of omnipotence and omniscience are themselves contradictory. Dawkins mentions this "discovery" of the logicians in *The God Delusion*. To para-phrase: So, if God knows what He is going to do tomorrow, then He doesn't have the power to do something different, does He? St. Thomas clears away many such misunderstand-ings, for example, by relating how God is eternal and beyond the restraints of time as we know it. You and I have a "tomor-row," but there is a sense in which everything is always present for God.

Consider, as a simple analogy, a man heading toward a town on a very hilly road. He cannot see beyond each of the hills as he comes upon them, while someone with a perspective from high above the earth can see the town the whole time, as well as each hill that he comes upon one by one, in succes-sion. In a similar vein, C. S. Lewis wrote that "if you picture Time as a straight line along which we have to travel, then you must picture God as the whole page on which the line is drawn."[7] While we must progress from point A through point B to arrive at point C, the whole line of yesterdays, todays, and tomorrows is always visible to God. He stands eternally outside the time line.

St. Thomas takes reason to its limits in understanding God, and he notes that we require divine revelation to go fur-ther. Reason, for example, can tell us of God's oneness and simplicity (not made of parts), His omnipotence, omniscience, and so on, but we know only through divine revelation that God is also *three*: Father, Son, and Holy Spirit. This remains a mystery. We cannot fully comprehend the Trinity with our reason, but neither is the Trinity inherently contradictory, as the profound considerations of thinkers from St. Augustine to St. Thomas have shown us.

And so, there is no doubt that St. Thomas's writings are full of philosophical and theological profundities. But there was something else that really drew me in, and that was the fact that his writings are so positive, practical, and useful. Professor Dawkins complains that "the Christian focus is overwhelmingly on sin sin sin sin sin sin sin" (yep, all of those "sins" are in *The God Delusion*).[8] Although St. Thomas does indeed write about sin, he devotes many hundreds of pages to the nature of the human soul, explaining how we think, and feel, and will, along with superb advice on how to perfect those abilities by acquiring human virtues. His focus is overwhelmingly, then, on *virtue virtue virtue virtue virtue virtue virtue* — and the end, or goal, of virtue is *happiness happiness happiness*... (okay, you get the idea). Indeed, my own previous books on memory improvement, physical and spiritual fitness, and cultivation of virtues all draw heavily from the "Second Part" of the *Summa Theologica* on Creation. It is in the "Third Part" of the *Summa Theologica* that St. Thomas examines what we learn from the Incarnation of Christ and the sacraments of His Church.

The Superman of Heart, Mind, and Soul

As you may recall, Seneca advised us to "set our affections on some good man and keep him constantly before our eyes, so that we may live as if he were watching us, and do everything as if he saw what we were doing."[9] To quote Seneca's great contemporary, Paul of Tarsus: "When I was a child, I spoke like a child, I thought like a child, I reasoned like a child: when I became a man, I gave up childish ways" (1 Cor 13:11).

The "good man" constantly before my eyes in childhood was Superman. He embodied strength, courage, and goodness — but of course, he wasn't real. A little later, Aristotle took that role, embodying for me the pinnacle of achievement of the human mind. (Remember, if you will, that in his book *Human Accomplishment*, modern social scientist Charles Murray is in complete agreement!) I kept my eyes on the three great Stoic teachers as well.

Years later, I encountered a gentle giant who stood on the shoulders of the mighty Aristotle and those Stoics as well, to get an even better view of a man who hung on a cross. This was St. Thomas Aquinas, and his role in this book is far from over. Just keep reading and you'll see why.

TRUTH BOX #9

Faith Has Its Reasons

"For when a man is ready to believe, he loves the truth he believes, he thinks out and takes to heart whatever reasons he can find in support thereof; and in this way human reason does not exclude the merit of faith but is a sign of greater merit."

St. Thomas Aquinas, *Summa Theologica*[10]

Those who portray Christian faith as belief without evidence (or "in the teeth" of the evidence) may not be aware that the first pope enjoined us to "always be prepared to make a defense... for the hope that is in you" (1 Pet 3:15). We Christians are to stand ready to explain the reasons for our beliefs. Further, the last words of that same verse instruct us to "do it with gentleness and reverence."

Hopefully, I haven't transgressed those Christian limits of gentleness and reverence with the atheists we've encountered in these pages. I haven't treated them with kid gloves, but neither have I donned the brass knuckles that some of today's new atheists seem to flash about with pride, if not "in the teeth of the evidence," then "in the teeth" of their "deluded" and intellectually impoverished theistic opponents, those who ascribe to a "failed hypothesis"[11] or to a God who is "not great."[12]

If these new atheists truly seek the truth, let them attack Christianity as it truly stands, not their impoverished representation of its unrepresentative extremes and historical errors. The Catholic Church, for one, has been a champion of reason for almost 2,000 years. And if the new atheists stand in such cognitive superiority over Catholics of limited intellectual endowment, then I wait with bated breath for their *Summa Scientifica*, showing us how to improve upon the lessons for loving and living provided by the Jewish carpenter and His angelic doctor.

CHAPTER 10

C. S. Lewis: God Save the Queen

"If you are a Christian you do not have to believe that all the other religions are simply wrong all through. If you are an atheist you do have to believe that the main point in all the religions of the whole world is simply one huge mistake."

C. S. LEWIS, *Mere Christianity*[1]

"Very well then, atheism is too simple. And I will tell you another view that is also too simple. It is the view I call Christianity-and-water, the view which simply says there is a good God in Heaven and everything is all right — leaving out all the difficult and terrible doctrines about sin and hell and the devil, and the redemption. Both these are boys' philosophies."

C. S. Lewis, *Mere Christianity*[2]

"If you are thinking of becoming a Christian, I warn you, you are embarking on something which is going to take the whole of you, brains and all."

C. S. Lewis, *Mere Christianity*[3]

Years ago, it was popular in America to point out intriguing coincidences and similarities in the lives and deaths of Presidents Abraham Lincoln and John F. Kennedy. All right, so I just did a Google search, and lo and behold, there are still plenty of sites out there. There are lists ranging from as few as 17 coincidences to as many as several dozen — and from coincidences as mundane as both last names having seven letters to those as interesting as the fact that Lincoln was killed in Ford's Theatre, while Kennedy was killed riding in a Lincoln made by the Ford Motor Company.

Now here's one that's not on their lists. It's just a coincidence, but it happens to relate to Lincoln, Kennedy, and two influential figures in this book. You see, on February 12, 1809, both Abraham Lincoln and Charles Darwin were born, and on November 22, 1963, both John F. Kennedy and C. S. Lewis died. Yet here I am talking about U.S. presidents, when our chapter title refers to the Queen of England. So let's move along to the real topic at hand.

Surprised by Lewis

Who would have thought in 1929 that a 31-year-old, Irish-born atheistic Oxford University professor of English would become one of the most famous Christians of the 20th century, revered by Protestants and Catholics alike, even honored with a feast day (November 22) in the U.S. Episcopal Church? Who would have thought that a childless man in his mid-50s would become one of the world's most successful writers of children's fantasy tales? His *Chronicles of Narnia* have sold more than 120 million copies and have been made into major motion pictures. And who would have thought that the contented middle-aged bachelor and author of *Surprised by Joy* would later be surprised by another joy, Joy Gresham — a Jewish American, former Marxist-atheist turned Christian through the influence of his own writings?

Lewis and Gresham were married at her hospital bedside in 1956, and four years later she succumbed to cancer. Lewis used a pen name to write *A Grief Observed*, in which he worked through the heart-wrenching loss, suffused with lessons for us all, on life, death, and suffering. After the urging of his friends to read this book, he finally made it known that he was indeed its *author*. A wonderful film adaptation of Lewis and Gresham's relationship, *Shadowlands*, was produced in 1993. Lewis had a life full of surprises, but he has provided that greatest of surprises for those millions of fortunate readers of his books.

Clive Staples (or "Jack," as he preferred) Lewis was born in Belfast, Ireland, on November 29, 1898. He was baptized into the Church of Ireland, became an atheist during his adolescent years, reverted to theism, and then to Christianity and the Church of England in his early 30s. Lewis became an author of worldwide renown, writing classics of Christian apologetics and ethics, literary criticism, fantasy tales, and even a science fiction trilogy. Both his fiction and nonfiction works were imbued with his Christian beliefs.

So how did C. S. Lewis factor into my own spiritual journey? I had read a few of Lewis's books during my adolescent immersion in Christianity. I recalled that his *Mere Christianity* was an enjoyable and well-written summary of some of the most important fundamentals on which the great majority of Christians could agree — things like the Trinity, the Incarnation, Christian morality, natural law, sin, forgiveness, and virtue. The book provided well-reasoned replies to atheism. But when I first read it, I was no atheist, and many of the arguments later slipped my mind. I also recall enjoying his science fiction trilogy — *Out of the Silent Planet*, *Perelandra*, and *That Hideous Strength* — along with a collection of theological essays entitled *God in the Dock*.

When I discovered the writings of the great atheists, the vast majority of the popular Christian books in my own library — including book after book by the guru of positive thinking, Dr. Norman Vincent Peale, upon which I fed daily in my teens — were cast by the wayside. I have them no longer. In 2004, when I came back to God, I was pleasantly surprised to see that Lewis's books, though neglected, were never discarded. I have them still, along with a fresh batch of new ones.

Sweet Dreams

Lewis wrote that "God designed the human machine to run on Himself."[4] God, through His love and His laws, is the answer to human longings and our only true fulfillment and means of complete happiness and joy. The tragedies of human history most often arise when God is neglected, and when cruel and selfish people gain control. At this point, "the machine conks" because we are running on "the juice" supplied by Satan, not God.[5]

Lewis notes, however, that God has provided several special guides to keep us on course. He has provided us with a conscience to tell right from wrong. He provided special guidance to one particular people, the Jews, "hammering into their heads"[6] the idea that He is One and that He wants us to be good. His ultimate guide for us occurred in that moment in history when He took on human flesh to walk among us and to forgive our sins. Lewis mentions one other guide *from* God that many atheists see as evidence *against* the existence of God, yet it is one of the guides that most powerfully pulled me back to Him, partly through C. S. Lewis.

This is where the "good dreams" come in. Critics of Christianity will often note that other, older religions and mythologies throughout the world talk about how a god dies and is reborn, providing salvation to mankind. They take this as evidence that Christianity is all made up and is not factually true. Well, Lewis sees these "queer," or unusual, stories as "good dreams" that God sent to the human race in preparation for the Incarnation.[7] Lewis, then, like Aquinas, has no fear of Greeks bearing gifts, nor of Romans, Egyptians, Indians, Babylonians, or anyone else. As St. Thomas drank from the philosophical wisdom of the ancient classical civilizations, so, too, did Lewis imbibe "to the point of hilarity"[8] from the rich and pleasing drafts of their mythologies.

This I liked. You see, when my heart and mind were turning back toward God and the Church five years ago, I had been drawn into the study of the ancient Greek and Latin languages, mostly out of love for Greek and Roman philosophy, especially Aristotle and the Stoics, as you well know. Indeed, I built quite a collection of books from Harvard University's Loeb Classical Library, delightful little books (green for Greek and red for Latin), with the original language text on the left-hand page and the English translation on the right. What I hadn't really considered when I also started stacking up Greek- and Latin-language learning books was that Greek was also the language of the New Testament, Latin the language of the Catholic Church, and that the Loeb library was also bristling with books by the ancient Greek and Latin Church Fathers — folks like St. Clement of Alexandria (a man of the second century A.D., as learned in the classical Greek as in the early Christian cultures), St. Augustine (a man of the fourth century, most learned in the classical Latin and Christian culture), as well as others like Eusebius of Caesarea (a Christian bishop of the early fourth century and the "Father of Church History").

Well, wasn't I in for an interesting lesson in language, history, and unexpectedly, in Christianity! Perhaps you've been taught, as most modern educated people have, that the Catholic Church squashed our classical Greco-Roman heritage, until secular humanists gave it "rebirth" in the "Renaissance" (from, roughly, the 14th century to the 17th century).

Actually, that's not quite the case. For one thing, many of the great works of the classical world had been saved and reproduced throughout the centuries within Catholic monasteries. Further, great theologians of the 13th century — most prominently St. Thomas Aquinas and his teacher St. Albert the Great — had long before mined the great classics of Greco-Roman philosophy for their wisdom.

In drawing upon the wisdom of the classical world, C. S. Lewis was perpetuating a Christian tradition that goes back to its very beginnings. St. Paul did the same. When I began to read Lewis again after a 20-year hiatus, I discovered, for one thing, his love for the Roman poet Virgil's great epic, the *Aeneid*, the first-century-B.C. story that continues Homer's *Iliad*, starting from the sack of Troy to the founding of Rome. I had just read the *Aeneid* for the first time and had been memorizing some of its magnificently sonorous opening lines in the original Latin (e.g., *"Arma virumque cano Troiae qui primus ab oris"* — "I sing a song of arms and of the man who first came from the shores of Troy"[9]). I also read for the first time Lewis's lesser known, though most intriguing *Till We Have Faces*, a fantasy that retells the ancient Greek myth of Cupid and Psyche.

(By the way, I do most of my reading with classical music playing quietly in the background, and one of my favorites is by the little-known, 19th-century classical composer Anton Bruckner. I happened to be listening to his hauntingly beautiful Mass No. 1 in D minor while reading this unusual and moving book. It was like having one of those good dreams — while awake. I highly recommend this particular reading/listening combination.)

And here is truly a most fortuitous writing/listening coincidence for you. As I type at this moment, it occurs to me that my computer's speakers are gracing my ears with Mozart's Symphony No. 40. Modern musicians have a very interesting way of remembering this one. Its striking opening notes are given the words, "It's a bird. It's a plane. It's a Mozart!" and it is jokingly referred to as Mozart's "Superman Symphony"!

No Safe Lion

Back now to C. S. Lewis. He is one of many great examples of the thinking man's Christian. As one of this chapter's opening quotations reveals, Lewis was quite aware that, despite the claims of the atheists, when we enter the door of a church, we need not leave our brains at the door. Lewis left us with many deeply thought-provoking books of Christian theology, apologetics, and devotion.

Among my favorites are *The Four Loves*, his examination of affection, friendship, erotic love, and charity — four of the greatest of God's gifts to us, and the greatest of gifts we can share with others. *The Screwtape Letters* is an ingenious collection of letters from a junior demon soliciting advice from his boss on how to best tempt and corrupt humans, to recruit them for hell. This book splendidly demonstrates Lewis's subtle mastery of human psychology, as does another of my personal favorites, *The Great Divorce*. This book has nothing to do with failed marriages, but addresses the great theological and psychological divide between heaven and hell. Here, a busload of people from hell take a day trip up to heaven. Lewis shows how completely and resolutely the folks down there, for their various individual reasons, had chosen their own destinies by their complete and resolute refusal to accept God's love and mercy. The dynamic interactions between those in heaven and their visitors from hell again reveal Lewis as a master of the workings of the human mind and soul.

But what about this "no safe lion" business? Well, I'm getting there. The classic triad sought and cherished by any real philosophy is that of *truth*, *goodness*, and *beauty*. C. S. Lewis, in his life and in his works, embodied all three most admirably. If you delve deeper into Lewis, please be sure, if possible, to watch the movie *Shadowlands*, to read as many of his books as possible, and to read good books about him.

One thing that stands out in bold relief is this man's goodness. For example, while serving in World War I, he and a friend, Edward "Paddy" Moore, made a pact that if either of them died, the other would take care of the survivor's family. Paddy did not make it back. He was killed in battle in 1918. When Lewis returned to England, he did indeed take care of Paddy's mother, Jane Moore. He lived with her for over 30 years and called her "mother." (His own mother had died of cancer in his early childhood.) When Jane later required placement in a nursing home due to dementia, Lewis visited her every day until her death in 1951. For another example, Lewis answered, in his own hand, thousands of letters from his readers over the course of many years. Further, half of the proceeds of his book sales were donated to charity. Lewis was indeed a superman of goodness.

As for the beautiful, simply read one of Lewis's books, fiction or nonfiction, and you'll see examples aplenty of Lewis's appreciation of the beauties of creation, as well as Lewis's own mastery of the beauties of English prose. And as for the true, Lewis's books — again, both his fiction and nonfiction — abound in the truth.

Regarding the truth of Christ, Lewis is well-known for his famous "trilemma." Reacting to some of the "Christianity-and-water" theologians of the mid-20th century who denied Christ's divinity, portraying Him as merely a "great moral teacher," Lewis argued that a mere man who went around proclaiming what Jesus did could be no great moral teacher. Indeed, he must either be "a lunatic — on a level with the man who says he is a poached egg," a "Devil of Hell," or God.[10] This trilemma has been alliteratively rendered by some as "Lunatic, Liar, or Lord." Richard Dawkins addresses this trilemma in *The God Delusion*, by the way. He offers a fourth alternative, that perhaps Jesus was simply "honestly mistaken."[11] Well, I stand most intrigued by the logic of his amateur psychodiagnostics. Billions of humans who *believe that God exists* are suffering from *delusions*, while a man who *believes that **he** is God* has simply made an *honest mistake!*

Okay, let's get back to the "L" words. Lewis has provided one more in his *Chronicles of Narnia*: lion. The animal hero of this fantasy series of seven books is a lordly lion named Aslan. Aslan allows himself to be sacrificed, and is resurrected, to triumph over evil and redeem the realm of Narnia. Aslan represents Jesus Christ, of course, and at one point in the book a child asks if Aslan is a safe lion, and the answer is: "Who said anything about safe? 'Course he isn't safe. But he's good. He's the King, I tell you."[12]

Lewis saw the true, the good, and the beautiful in Jesus Christ, and he recognized that meekness must not be confused with weakness. Christ was crucified not because of His weakness, but went to the cross most bravely and willingly, despite His unspeakable strength. And while the meek follower of Christ may willingly bear his own cross — as did the divine sacrificial Lamb — there are times when he must stand up, speak out, and act for others in a most boldly and leonine fashion! Christ himself did not spare His words or actions for the "brood of vipers" and moneychangers who defiled his Father's temple.

Mere Christianity includes a chapter on the classical "cardinal virtues," including *prudence* (practical wisdom), *temperance* (self-control), and *justice* (fairness). These virtues — in addition to the special God-given "theological virtues" of *faith, hope,* and *charity* — are the stuff of which Christian lives are made. Aslan — that good, but *unsafe* lion — reminds us all of that fourth cardinal virtue of *fortitude*, or courage. Fortitude bears all manner of adversity in achieving hard-won goals. It faces and endures difficult and sometimes painful things, even unto martyrdom in some. The related concept of courage comes from the Latin word *cor*, for heart. And so, C. S. Lewis — that good, loving, pipe-smoking English gentleman — reminds us that, as Christians, we must boldly and courageously serve God with all of self — heart and mind, body and soul.

TRUTH BOX #10

A Moral Argument

Humans possess a basic, fundamental sense of right and wrong that argues for the existence of God.

This basic idea underlies one of C. S. Lewis's core arguments for God's existence — and yet some, especially today, argue not only that such a sense *does not argue for* God's existence, but that it argues *against* it. Others even argue that *humans do not possess such a fundamental sense of right and wrong*!

Christopher Hitchens argues that even atheists have this inborn moral sense of basic right and wrong — so who needs God?

It really is true that atheists can strive to live lives of moral virtue. The difference of opinion here is *where* that moral sense comes from. No animals outside of man possess it, since they are guided by instinct, not by an intellectual and volitional morality. Christians hold that we have been created in God's image, and it is through His gift to us that our human nature images His capacity to know the true and to will the good.

Today, extreme multiculturalists and moral relativists will argue that there is no such fundamental moral sense (as

Bertrand Russell did likewise decades ago). Different cultures have different mores and values and taboos after all. Some cultures believe in polygamy and in the subjugation of women, for example. So how can we believe that morality comes from God and that we can impose our morality on others? And look at the controversy over the Ten Commandments. Aren't they limited to a Judeo-Christian view of the world?

Well, it's time to wrap up this chapter, but let's learn once again from a very prominent enemy of Christianity. Roman Emperor Julian the Apostate admitted in *Against the Galileans* that the last seven commandments (those dealing with man's interactions with man) were obviously universally valid across cultures and throughout history.

CHAPTER 11

G. K. Chesterton: What Could Be Right With the World

"The Christian ideal has not been tried and found wanting. It has been found difficult and left untried."
G. K. CHESTERTON, *What's Wrong With the World*[1]

"I never dreamed that the Roman religion was true; but I knew that its accusers, for some reason or other, were curiously inaccurate."
G. K. CHESTERTON,
The Catholic Church and Conversion[2]

"I had no more idea of becoming a Catholic than of becoming a cannibal. I imagined that I was merely pointing out that justice should be done even to cannibals."
G. K. CHESTERTON,
The Catholic Church and Conversion[3]

"Our enemies no longer really know how to attack the faith; but that is no reason why we should not know how to defend it."
G. K. CHESTERTON,
The Catholic Church and Conversion[4]

I ask you, what is wrong with the world? (The world of Catholic education, that is.) How could a bookish, Catholic grade school academic-scholarship winner go through four more years of Catholic high school, and a year of Catholic college, and not know G. K. Chesterton from the man in the moon? Chesterton appears near the end of this book because he came on the stage quite late in my own reversion scenario. Until I was drawn back into the Church in my early 40s, G. K. Chesterton stood out in my mind as one of those witty literary fellows they like to feature in books of quotable quotes — pretty much a British Mark Twain, he was, in my estimation. Though he came in late, Chesterton had an uncanny ability to turn back the clock, and now it's time to see how he did it for me.

Turning Back the Clock

I read my first book by Gilbert Keith Chesterton (1874-1936) in 2004. It is called *What's Wrong with the World* (1910), and he really tells us, while pulling no punches. He takes on issues relevant to family life, to newly emerging theories of feminism, and he even introduces us to the foibles of one Mr. Hudge (big business) and Mr. Gudge (big government), arguing for a locally-governed alternative to both capitalism and socialism called "distributism" (also known as "distributivism" and "distributionism"). Chesterton had been a socialist in his youth, yet he would later go on to debate prominent socialistic thinkers of his day, including our own Lord Bertrand Russell of Chapter 2, whom Gilbert Keith informed: "No society can survive the socialist fallacy that there is an absolutely unlimited number of inspired officials and an absolutely unlimited amount of money to pay them."[5]

Chesterton was not just one for punching and finger pointing, though. When the esteemed British paper *The Times* once invited preeminent authors to write on the theme "What's Wrong With the World?" Chesterton replied with a brief letter:

Dear Sirs,

I am.

Sincerely,

G.K. Chesterton[6]

Chesterton, you see, realized some things about human nature, both in its grandeur and in its limitations, and he knew these limitations applied to himself as much as to anyone else. So, as I dipped into my first Chesterton book, I got a glimpse of the great man's brilliant social and economic analysis, as well as his inimitable writing style.

He had an incredible knack for turning supposedly common-sense sayings inside-out and topsy-turvy in thought-provoking paradox after thought-provoking paradox. Indeed, Chesterton's book on Christ, *The Everlasting Man*, was acknowledged by no less than C. S. Lewis as one of the main influences that eventually led him to abandon atheism and embrace Christ.

Chesterton shares with other great Christian thinkers a boldness and freshness of thought, coupled with a humility born of wisdom that does not presume to cast aside the genius of great thinkers and great traditions of the past. Chesterton always questioned the popular assumptions of his day, inspired in part by then-fresh evolutionary theory and the idea that humanity was on a road to unlimited progress and improvement. And so, when Chesterton saw some very negative social trends developing in the early 20th century — the era that brought us anarchists, Bolsheviks, World War I, and more — he responded to the tired cliché, that you can't reverse progress or "turn back the clock," with the statement that setting back the hands of a clock is among the easiest possible things we can do: just adjust the knobs in the back or the hands themselves in the front. He knew, of course, that we can't turn back time itself, but we can recreate any man-made thing or system that was created in the past. Chesterton's own ideas helped set back the hands of my own theological clock, and it hasn't stopped ticking since.

A Great Big Man With Many Tomes

Chesterton stood 6 feet 4 inches tall and tipped the Toledo Scale at approximately 300 pounds. This mustachioed, bespectacled giant cut a most impressive figure when donning his massive overcoat, cape, hat, cigar, swordstick, and revolver when traversing the streets of London, where he worked as a newspaper journalist. And he was as prolific as he was large. He wrote nearly 80 books, hundreds of articles, and thousands of essays. He authored great classics of Catholic apologetics, detective stories (the *Father Brown* stories), scads of newspaper commentaries, poetry, and much more. I've read but a smattering of his works thus far — which gives me all the more reason to look forward to years of reading pleasure ahead.

After *What's Wrong with the World*, I read Chesterton's book about another gentle, genius giant of Catholicism, his biography of our hero of Chapter 9, St. Thomas Aquinas. The story goes that when Chesterton sat down to write this book, he spent a short time thumbing through a stack of books on St. Thomas that his secretary had brought to him. He then set them aside and wrote his book. My own favorite book explaining the intricacies of the weighty philosophy of St. Thomas — including those famous proofs of the existence of God — is *The Christian Philosophy of St. Thomas Aquinas*, by the profound French Thomist philosopher Etienne Gilson. Gilson himself reported that what G. K. Chesterton had whipped together was the greatest of all the biographies of St. Thomas. Chesterton captured so delightfully both the intellectual profundity and the humble simplicity of this ever-so-saintly super sage.

I've also read Chesterton's apologetic classics *The Everlasting Man, Orthodoxy,* and *The Catholic Church and Conversion,* as well as his intriguing novel *The Man Who Was Thursday.* It's hard to describe Chesterton's writing style if you've never read him. His books brim over with delightfully unexpected twists and turns. Ironically, this man who cautioned us not to get carried away with the concept of "progress" was definitely "a man ahead of his time."

Just for kicks, I did an Internet search of "Chesterton Dawkins." Bearing in mind that the portly British Catholic Chesterton died five years before the svelte British "Bright" Dawkins was born, I found several postings wherein quotations from godly Gilbert had answered in advance, with warm words of wise wit, several of poor Richard's all-but-maniacal, materialistic mutterings. In one compare-and-contrast quote from his book *Climbing Mount Improbable,* Dawkins, replying to his own daughter's statement that wildflowers exist so that the world will be pretty and bees can make us honey, explains to her (with sorrow) that she is wrong, and that they really exist *for* the benefit of one thing only — "DNA."[7] The contrasting Chesterton quote from *Orthodoxy* includes the following:

> Because children have abounding vitality, because they are in spirit fierce and free, therefore they want things repeated and unchanged. They always say, "Do it again"; and the grown-up person does it again until he is nearly dead. For grown-up people are not strong enough to exult in monotony. But perhaps God is strong enough to exult in monotony. It is possible that God says every morning, "Do it again" to the sun; and every evening, "Do it again" to the moon. It may not be automatic necessity that makes all daisies alike; it may be that God makes every daisy separately, but has never got tired of making them. It may be that He has

the eternal appetite of infancy; for we have sinned and grown old, and our Father is younger than we. The repetition in Nature may not be a mere recurrence; it may be a theatrical *encore*.[8]

Christ said we must become as children to enter the king-dom of God. This does not mean we must become ignorant and naïve, but that we must be receptive and open to the awe-some wonder of the universe and its ever more awesomely won-drous Creator. I would also like to offer this reply (originally penned by Chesterton) to the new atheists who wax elegant about DNA as the ultimate biological reality:

Oh, I admit that you have your case and have it by heart, and that many things do fit into other things as you say. I admit that your explanation explains a great deal; but what a great deal it leaves out![9]

And here is one more Chestertonian chestnut that one blogger considers a delightful answer in advance to our joyless breed of new atheists:

If you argue with a madman, it is extremely probable that you will get the worst of it; for in many ways his mind moves all the quicker for not being delayed by the things that go with good judgement. He is not hampered by a sense of humour or by charity, or by the dumb certainties of experience. He is the more logical for losing certain sane affections. Indeed, the common phrase for insanity is in this respect a misleading one. The madman is not the man who has lost his reason. The madman is the man who has lost everything ex-cept his reason.[10]

Chesterton, you see, was not only a physical giant, but a lit-erary and intellectual titan as well. No Roman Catholic of "less than normal intelligence" was he. He was so well aware that, as far as heresies and fallacies go, there is really nothing new under the sun. Two thousand years worth of great minds, guided by the Holy Spirit, have considered and refuted virtually every sort of materialistic, reductionistic approach to the universe, time and again over the centuries. In his book *Heresies*, and interspersed throughout his voluminous writings, Chesterton addressed a great number of these ever-recurring fallacies and misconceptions, always with wisdom and panache.

A Great Big House With Many Rooms

Throughout his youth and young adulthood, Chesterton had toyed with various political and spiritual belief systems, dabbling in paganism, agnosticism, socialism, and spiritualism, to name a few. But as the years went by and he grew in knowledge and experience (as well as in manly girth), Chesterton came to find himself defending again and again the perennial spiritual and worldly wisdom of the Catholic Church. For example, in seeking a humane middle ground between the excesses of socialism and of unbridled capitalism, Chesterton found true wisdom in the late-19th-century encyclicals of Pope Leo XIII (the great champion of St. Thomas Aquinas we encountered briefly in Chapter 9) on issues such as socialism, capitalism, and human liberty.

But what about houses and rooms? Oh, yes, let's go first to the house of C. S. Lewis. One of the wonderful metaphors in his *Mere Christianity* is his depiction of organized Christianity as a house of many rooms. Those fundamentals of the faith held in agreement by the vast majority who call themselves "Christian" — things such as the theology of the Trinity and the Incarnation and the classic Christian virtues — exist in the hall of a great house with many rooms. Each room represents a different denomination of the Christian Church, and it is up to each of us to ask, "Which door is the true one?"[11] Thirty-five years before the publication of Lewis's *Mere Christianity*, Chesterton had written his own book dealing with the core "mere" issues of Lewis's hallway. *Orthodoxy* addresses those same essential fundamentals of the Christian faith, without addressing the "very fascinating" question of who on earth possesses the authority to promulgate this faith.[12]

Unlike Lewis, Chesterton later did indeed come to discuss that "very fascinating" question of authority. Of course, for a man as large as Chesterton, one room would not do, so he chose the whole house. *The Catholic Church and Conversion* (1926), published four years after his conversion, explains how his search for truth and for true freedom and liberation (from sin) led him there. This book I have written lacks the square footage to begin to hold Chesterton's words of wisdom on the authority, majesty, and fullness of truth within the Catholic Church. For that, I refer you to his own books. In the next chapter, we will discuss the second-to-last man to sit in that very "seat of authority" for that Church. But first, let's revisit the Superman one more time, with G. K. Chesterton himself as our guide. Indeed, you will see that Chesterton *almost* shook his hand!

How Chesterton Found the Superman

Chesterton lived when the possible social implications of the theory of evolution were experiencing their first heyday. Some thinkers argued that the concept of "the survival of the fittest" was as apt a guide to man's ethical choices as it was a cause of his biological structure. Many of these same thinkers discussed the possibilities of selective human breeding to purposefully produce a race of super men and women (and to reduce the reproductive activities of the racially, ethnically, and socially "undesirable"). Sir Francis Galton, a pioneer in the study of human intelligence and a half-cousin of Charles Darwin, coined the term "eugenics" (from the Greek, meaning, literally, "good genes") and encouraged such selective human breeding. Among those to derive inspiration from Galton's work on human eugenics were two of Chesterton's contemporaries: Margaret Sanger, founder and "great hero"[13] of Planned Parenthood, and Adolf Hitler, failed founder of the "Master Race."

What does Chesterton, the Caped Crusader of Catholicism, have to do with "the Superman?" Well, in 1909, he wrote a little piece for *The Daily News* (not to be confused with *The Daily Planet*) entitled "How I Met the Superman"[14] — Chesterton's debate antagonist George Bernard Shaw had written a popular play, *Man and Superman*, several years earlier.

(As you read the following synopsis of Chesterton's article, please keep in mind that, while he points out real truths, the events in his little parable would appear to be purely fictional. And see if you find, as I think I have found, shadows of Ms. Sanger and Sir Francis in there as well!)

To begin, journalist Chesterton has received a scoop on the whereabouts of the Superman, who is residing at the home of his parents. His mother, the former Lady Hypatia Smyth-Brown, was once a determined social reformer whose greatest ambition was, in her own words, "protecting the poor from themselves."

One day, when removing an offensive "oleograph" (perhaps a religious picture?) from the bedroom wall of a female Irish apple peddler, Lady Hypatia was struck upon the head with an umbrella by this "ignorant and partly intoxicated Celt." This blow prompted a fit of mental illness, during which Lady Hypatia consented to marry Dr. Hagg, a world-renowned eugenicist, thus becoming Lady Hagg.

Dr. Hagg had "achieved that bold and bright outlook upon the future of Socialism which only geology can give." And so, Dr. Hagg could proclaim that, according to the dictates of the survival of the fittest, the poor should not be protected — in fact, "the weakest must go to the wall." In any event, "the result is that this union of the two highest types of our civilisation, the fashionable lady and all but vulgar medical man, has been blessed by the birth of the Superman...."

Our intrepid journalist, upon finding the home of the now-15-year-old Superman, asks to see the wondrous child. The super parents, however, are mysteriously reluctant to let this happen. So Chesterton starts questioning them.

"Has he got any hair?" They hem and haw.

"Is he nice looking?"

"He creates his own standard, you see," replies the mother, then adds, ending with a sigh: "Upon that plane he is more than Apollo."

Chesterton, pressing on, asks more questions.

"If it isn't hair... is it feathers?" Again, there is no clear answer.

Chesterton, now growing irritated, asks again if he can see him: "I should like to say that I had shaken hands with the Superman." The mother reports that due to her child's structure, he can't exactly shake hands.

At this point, Chesterton bursts into the Superlad's pitch-dark bedroom, and then hears a weak yelp and a piercing "double shriek" behind him. He has unwittingly let in a draft, and the Superman is dead.

As Chesterton leaves the home that evening, men carry out a small coffin "that was not of any human shape," while the winds howl vigorously. "It is, indeed," says Dr. Hagg, "the whole universe weeping over the frustration of its most magnificent birth." But, muses Chesterton, "I thought that there was a hoot of laughter in the high wail of the wind."

So ends Chesterton's parable of the eugenic, man-made Superman. Let's move next to a very recent, very profound, and indeed very super... pope.

TRUTH BOX #11

Recent Writers Right About God

"Seek and you will find." (Lk 11:9)

G. K. Chesterton was a wonderful apologist, revealing the greatness of Christ and the Catholic Church. I strongly recommend that you seek and find his great books. Here, though, I would like to provide you with a list of some of the modern books that I found most helpful in preparing for writing this one.

For additional background on some of the old-school atheists, I recommend Donald De Marco and Benjamin Wiker's *Architects of the Culture of Death*; Wiker's *10 Books that Screwed Up the World: And 5 Others That Didn't Help*; and Paul C. Vitz's *Faith of the Fatherless: The Psychology of Atheism*. Anglican molecular biophysicist and theologian Alister McGrath has addressed the new atheists in several good books including *The Twilight of Atheism: The Rise and Fall of Disbelief in the Modern World*; *Dawkins' God: Genes, Memes, and the Meaning of Life*; and *The Dawkins Delusion? Atheistic Fundamentalism and the Denial of the Divine*.

Books addressing issues of materialism, atheism, the proper limits of evolutionary theory, as well as intelligent design theory, all from a Catholic perspective, include George Sim Johnston's *Did Darwin Get it Right? Catholics and the Theory of Evolution*; Scott Hahn and Benjamin Wiker's *Answering the New Atheism: Dismantling Dawkins' Case Against God*; Michael J. Behe's *Darwin's Black Box: The Biochemical Challenge to Evolution* and *The Edge of Evolution: The Search for the Limits of Darwinism*; Father Thomas D. Williams'

Greater Than You Think: A Theologian Answers the Atheists About God; and Christoph Cardinal Schönborn's *Chance or Purpose? Creation, Evolution, and a Rational Faith* and *Creation and Evolution: A Conference with Pope Benedict XVI in Castel Gandolfo.*

Two great books by a prominent Christian scientist and a prominent former atheistic philosopher are Francis S. Collins's *The Language of God: A Scientist Presents Evidence for Belief* and Antony Flew's *There Is a God: How the World's Most Notorious Atheist Changed His Mind* (I enjoyed the latter one immensely).

To experience the intellectual fireworks that ensue when a Dominican Thomist confronts a materialistic Darwinist, be sure not to miss *God Is No Delusion: A Refutation of Richard Dawkins,* by Father Thomas Crean, O.P.

Finally, although it's not a book, I also heartily endorse Ben Stein's movie *Expelled: No Intelligence Allowed* as an eye-opener/thought-provoker.

CHAPTER 12

Pope John Paul II: Faith and Reason, Body and Soul

"Faith and reason are like two wings on which the human spirit rises to the contemplation of truth; and God has placed in the human heart a desire to know the truth — in a word, to know himself — so that, by knowing and loving God, men and women may also come to the fullness of truth about themselves (cf. Ex 33:18; Ps 27:8-9; 63:2-3; Jn 14:8; 1 Jn 3:2)."

POPE JOHN PAUL II, *Fides et Ratio*[1]

"The fool thinks that he knows many things, but really he is incapable of fixing his gaze on the things that truly matter. Therefore he can neither order his mind (Prov 1:7) nor assume a correct attitude to himself or to the world around him. And so when he claims that 'God does not exist' (cf. Ps 14:1), he shows with absolute clarity just how deficient his knowledge is and just how far he is from the full truth of things, their origin and their destiny."

POPE JOHN PAUL II, *Fides et Ratio*[2]

"It is the one and the same God who establishes and guarantees the intelligibility and reasonableness of the natural order of things upon which scientists confidently depend and who reveals himself as the Father of our Lord Jesus Christ."

POPE JOHN PAUL II, *Fides et Ratio*[3]

It was August or September of 1978 and a high school buddy was doing a pretty nice job of mimicking some very impressive-sounding Latin phrases. Neither of us had studied Latin. I took French, and I'm not sure if he studied a foreign language at all, but we knew that the words blaring forth from the radio sounded as important as they were sonorous. As I think back more than 30 years later, I'm not sure if we were listening to Pope John Paul I or Pope John Paul II at the time. John Paul I became pope on August 26, 1978, only to be succeeded by Pope John II a month and a half later on October 16, after the former's untimely death on September 28. I also now realize that we really didn't have a clue about the true importance of those words. It would be more than a quarter of a century before I would read my first papal encyclical.

Fast-forward to April 2005: Perhaps a million people were packed together tightly, with thousands of them chanting a name in Italian — "Giovanni Paolo!" This time I knew who they were talking about. When, in the fall of 2004, my parish had started planning a trip to Rome, little did we realize that we would arrive during the week of the largest funeral gathering in Christian history. Pope John Paul II, the Pontifex Maximus, the earthly bridge to God, had crossed that bridge himself. Indeed, his last words, translated from Polish, were: "Let me go to the house of the Father."

It was only about a year before the pope's death that I started to realize what a great man he was. And even now, the more I learn of him, the more that realization grows.

The Philosopher Pope

Plato wrote of the benevolent philosopher kings, and Marcus Aurelius was one of them. With the death of John Paul II, the world lost a benevolent philosopher pope. Lo, had I been aware of John Paul II's profound grasp of things philosophical, as well as things theological, I wouldn't have been trying to fly on the one wing of reason for so long!

Karol Józef Wojtyła was born on May 18, 1920. He went on to study philosophy in college and was ordained a priest at age 26. Thirty-two years later, the philosophical cleric became our first pontiff from Poland. During a papacy of nearly 27 years, Pope John Paul II would become known for many things: his worldwide travels; his spirit of ecumenism, reaching out to non-Catholic Christians and to non-Christian religious believers as well (the Dali Llama met with him eight times); his revitalization of the Catholic youth of the world (many of whom proudly proclaim themselves as part of the "JP II generation"); his survival of an assassination attempt and, later, his act of forgiving his attacker in person; and his role in freeing Eastern Europe of communism. Some day he may become the fourth pope in history to be proclaimed "the Great" — and rightly so.

John Paul II fits into my own story, as I noted, rather late. Had I been aware of his grasp of Thomistic philosophy (and of phenomenology, which studies the subjective experience of the individual) a decade or two earlier, I could have written this book years ago — but without so many of the chapters in Part I! John Paul has given us a massive body of writings, including 14 encyclicals. I'll be focusing primarily here on his 13th encyclical, *Fides et Ratio* (on the relationship between faith and reason), written in 1998.

In *Fides et Ratio*, John Paul carries to the dawn of the 21st century those fundamental messages brought home so strongly by St. Thomas Aquinas in the 13th century: that God endowed man with reason for a reason; that man requires faith as well as reason; that though faith and reason have their own realms and their own limits, they do not contradict each another, but point to the same truths. While St. Thomas reconciled faith with ancient classical philosophy (especially that of Aristotle), John Paul II faced the task of reconciling faith with modern philosophy, and also with a veritable new religion to some: science.

The Fullness of Truth

Pope John Paul II encouraged us to seek out "the fullness of truth." The modern world is awash in a vast sea of truths, of scientific and historical data, of technological know-how, and of information of every imaginable kind. Knowledge is power, and this information explosion in the last few centuries has undoubtedly advanced greatly our abilities to shape the world and to control our destinies on this planet. These advances are primarily the fruits of science and technology.

John Paul II was certainly no enemy of scientific and technological knowledge, as a quick glance at his writings will show. Indeed, as he states, "one may define the human being… as the one who seeks the truth."[4] These kinds of factual and scientific pieces of truth do not tell the whole story, however. In *Fides et Ratio*, John Paul II reminds us of a uniquely human thinking capacity that rises even above knowledge — namely, that of *wisdom*.

Wisdom seeks answers not only to questions of how things work or how we can change things, but to questions like "Who am I?" and "Why am I here?" and "What does it mean to live a good life?" John Paul II notes that all cultures have addressed these questions in one way or another, as in the great religions of the East, and in the ancient epics and mythologies of the West. The Bible itself contains a rich "wisdom" literature, exhorting man to wisdom and praising God for the gifts that it brings: "Blessed is the man who meditates on wisdom and who reasons intelligently" (Sir 14:20). Approximately 2,500 years ago in classical Greece, a special discipline arose that was devoted to the study of wisdom, deriving from *philos* (love) and *sophia* (wisdom) — *philosophy* being "the love of wisdom."

The new atheists speak of a conflict between science and religion, proclaiming that science represents reason and intelligence, while religion represents faith and ignorance, and that we must choose one or the other. There is, however, a field of human knowledge that examines even the workings of science from a higher vantage point, and that field is philosophy. Part of the scientific method includes the creation of self-consistent and non-contradictory theories to explain empirical data (factual observations). Well, the laws of *logical reasoning* do not belong to the field of science itself but to philosophy. Philosophy can also examine data that a purely materialistic science must ignore or write off as a cumbersome by-product of atoms and genes — namely, human interior experience, or what it means to be you or to be me. Further, philosophy can address questions of what we "should" do, as well as what we "can" do. Science can tell us, for example, how to make deadly weapons, while philosophy can address whether, and under what circumstances, it might or might not be right to use them. This is part of the reason why John Paul II warns against misunderstanding the limits of science, of a "*scientism*" that thinks we need only concern ourselves with material facts, and not with the ethical implications of those facts (for *ethics*, too, is a branch of philosophy):

> In the field of scientific research, a positivistic mentality took hold which not only abandoned the Christian vision of the world, but more especially rejected every appeal to a metaphysical or moral vision. It follows that certain scientists, lacking any ethical point of reference, are in danger of putting at the center of their concerns something other than the human person and the entirety of the person's life.[5]

Philosophy can examine religion as well as science. John Paul II also warns against a "*fideism*," "which fails to recognize the importance of rational knowledge and philosophical discourse for the understanding of faith, indeed for the very possibility of belief in God."[6] We see this most commonly in "*biblicism*," which makes the Bible "the sole criterion of truth."[7] *Indeed, it is often this faith-only, fideistic approach of biblicism that the Darwinian new atheists attack as representative of Christian thought.* This idea warrants a little closer look, through the glasses of John Paul II himself.

The Evolution of a Pope

Rationalism and scientism versus fideism and biblicism is the stuff of American debates of "evolution vs. creationism." An introduction to the contest might sound something like this:

> "Ladies and Gentlemen: In this corner, from an Ivy League university, wearing a white laboratory coat and holding a model of the DNA double helix, stands the theory of the gradual evolution of mankind over the course of the 13-plus billion years of the universe. And in this corner, from the foothills of Appalachia, clad in a 19th-century parson's suit and wielding a very well-thumbed King James Version of the Bible, stands apparently the only viable option, that of a universe created four or five thousand years ago during a period of six calendar days."[8]

This false match-up, of course, leaves the views of the Catholic Church at ringside. Sixteen hundred years ago, St. Augustine wrote that the book of Genesis is not to be read as a literal guide to the step-by-step creation of the physical universe, or as Catholic theologian and physicist Father Stanley

Jaki put it more recently, the Bible does not teach us "how the heavens go, but how to go to heaven."[9]

But what would our modern philosophical pope in search of "the fullness of truth" make of this false matchup? We don't have to speculate, because John Paul II addressed the issue on October 22, 1996, when he addressed the Pontifical Academy of Sciences with a brief talk entitled "Truth Cannot Contradict Truth." He noted that 50 years earlier, Pope Pius XII had addressed the "hypothesis" of evolution and noted that it need not conflict with Christian faith unless it were to be over-interpreted as the whole truth about the origins and nature of man, in soul as well as in body. In other words, there is nothing to prevent God from choosing to create a universe with creatures that unfold, change, and evolve.

In John Paul II's view at that time, he considered that the evidence had mounted from so many independent quarters that the idea of evolution had become more than a mere "hypothesis" and could be considered a legitimate, supported theory. Here, though, he made some very important qualifiers, noting again that it is philosophy's role (including the special philosophical discipline of *epistemology*, the study of human knowledge itself) to evaluate theories. Further, he noted that evolution was, properly speaking, a matter of *theories*, in the plural, since there are competing explanations of the mechanisms of evolution among scientists — but more importantly, because there are various conflicting philosophies based upon it. Dawkins and the new atheists, for example, interpret evolution as evidence for a purely materialistic view of the universe, implying that the spiritual and the concept of the soul are but delusions.

Here John Paul II definitely begs to differ. He cites St. Thomas Aquinas's profound insights on the way that man and man alone was created by God in His image, in terms of His *intellect* and His *will*. Materialists argue that we differ from other species not in manner, but only in degree. In *Fides et Ratio*, the pope points out that this fundamental truth of our existence was also apparent to the great champions of reason of the past. One of ancient philosophy's most famous injunctions was "Know thyself." This was inscribed on the temple of the ancient Greek oracle at Delphi. We human beings are the only creatures capable of seeking to know our own selves, as well as the One who made us.

On Two Wings and a Prayer

Pope John Paul II, then, flew to magnificent heights because he had so fully developed both of his "wings," the wing of faith and the wing of reason. The same man who chided modern theologians for ignoring classical philosophy, and modern philosophers for doubting the power of reason, spent hours each day in fervent prayer, devoutly loved the Virgin Mary, and canonized hundreds of holy people. The same man who championed the power of the human *mind* gleaned for us, from the book of Genesis and from the Gospels of Christ, a profound and beautiful theology of the *body*, sharing sublime lessons on masculinity and femininity as well as the true loving relationship between the sexes. Unlike Nietzsche, he knew that woman was made for far more than the recreation of the warrior. Unlike Rand, he knew that woman was made not to worship man, but to *love* him — and together, to worship *their* Creator. Unlike, Dawkins, he knew that it's about so much more than DNA!

John Paul II has left us a magnificent legacy in his writings, volumes of guidance to become wiser, more thoughtful human beings — and perhaps even more importantly, more loving people. Bertrand Russell said that love and knowledge were his goals. Those are goals that Pope John Paul II achieved like very few before him, and he's inspired millions to hope and pray and strive for the same, giving it their all, in faith and in reason, in mind and in body, in heart and in soul.

TRUTH BOX #12

A Champion of Truth

Without life, there can be no truth.

Pope John Paul II was as tireless a champion of life as he was a champion of truth. If truth is the correct correspondence between perception and reality, thought and thing, then it takes a living being to experience it! John Paul II fought tirelessly against what he called "the culture of death." Many in our modern world have come to deny the truth of the fundamental value and rights of every single human person, from conception until natural death. For example, the mother's womb (that most special and safest of all places, crafted to nourish and nurture new human life) has now become one of the most dangerous places on earth — and most often by the willful consent of the would-be mother and father, though they most likely do not perceive the truth of the evil they are committing.

In a culture of death, many parents have been inculturated to perceive abortion as a morally neutral, medical decision. We are not the first culture of death, of course. In ancient Greece, undesired babies could be exposed on the hillside, like the baby Oedipus, made so famous by Sophocles and later by Sigmund Freud. And just as the ancient Roman father had the legal right of life and death over his children, and just as the position of the emperor's thumb settled the fate of gladiators, so also the modern would-be mother now possesses a similar power of life and death over the baby inside her. Should we then feel any moral superiority over those who came before us (and before the message of Christ)?

Richard Dawkins does address the issue of abortion in *The God Delusion*, by the way. The issue for Dawkins is not whether the unborn child is "human" or a "person," but whether or not he or she can feel pain. Of course, whether it hurts or not, abortion definitely kills. And if pain is our main concern, then anesthetized mercy killings could very easily ensure that only the fittest among us survive.

Pope John Paul II embraced the wisdom of Thomism, which integrates the truth of both reason and faith. So, too, did he embrace the phenomenological philosophy that focuses on the unique experience and dignity of absolutely each and every human person. He knew that true knowledge and true love do not seek to eliminate the weakest and most dependent among us. His Teacher had taught him as a child: "As you did it to one of the least of these my brethren, you did it to me" (Mt 25:40).

The Real Superman

And the Word became flesh and dwelt among us, full of grace and truth; we have beheld his glory, glory as of the only-begotten Son from the Father.

JOHN 1:14

This unity of truth, natural and revealed, is embodied in a living and personal way in Christ, as the Apostle reminds us: "Truth is in Jesus" (cf. Eph 4:21; Col 1:15-20). He is the eternal Word in whom all things were created, and he is the incarnate Word who in his entire person reveals the Father (cf. Jn 1:14, 18). What human reason seeks "without knowing it" (cf. Acts 17:23) can be found only through Christ: what is revealed in him is "the full truth" (cf. Jn 1:14-16) of everything which was created in him and through him and which therefore in him finds its fulfillment (cf. Col 1:17).

POPE JOHN PAUL II, *Fides et Ratio*[1]

Friedrich Nietzsche recognized within us a will to power, and he saw it as a will to conquer and subdue. He considered the Christian who seeks to conquer and subdue his own weakness as weak and self-sacrificing, yet he urged us to think not of ourselves, but to prepare the way for some ruthless "superman" who will have moved "beyond good and evil" in the future.

Bertrand Russell said that knowledge and love should be our goals, but he was quick to discredit the knowledge of the great minds that preceded him and to define love within his own idiosyncratic and changing parameters.

Albert Ellis considered hedonism — the pursuit of long-range pleasures — as the most rational of our goals, yet he considered the pursuit of eternal bliss irrational.

Ayn Rand acknowledged man's mind and reason as the highest of all values, with love reserved for those who should prove themselves worthy of it.

Richard Dawkins seeks human perfection through scientific understanding, striving to raise our level of consciousness through acceptance of a materialistic philosophy that denies special significance to consciousness itself.

Nietzsche had his superman, Russell had mathematics, Rand had logic, Ellis had pleasure, and Dawkins has Darwin and evolution. What they all lack, of course, is merely the Creator of all power, knowledge, joy, reason, and of all living forms.

Alfred Adler came near to Him. To strive for superiority (for ourselves) and for social interest (for others) is much indeed like loving one's neighbor as one's self, and this is the *second* of the two great commandments. Adler, however, saw the giver (and the object) of the *first* great commandment as a fiction, man's own creation and model.[2]

Our Stoic sages were really on to something — lots of things, actually. Virtue is higher than pleasure and, indeed, produces deeper pleasures of its own. The most important power that human knowledge can produce is power over our own selves, and over our own attitudes, goals, and behaviors. We must also acknowledge the limits of our knowledge and our power, staying ever mindful of the vast order of things that surpass our knowledge and capacities, but which lie within the capacity of a Higher Power, a power the Stoics came to call Nature, Zeus, Fate — or God.

Mortimer Adler classed himself with such "pagan" philosophers for most of his life, acknowledging the existence of some kind of God — until later in life, when he learned His name.

Worldly Men

We can learn a great deal from great thinkers, even when their thinking goes awry. Each has some positive insight to provide us, and each has his or her group of devoted followers. The problems come in when their answers to *pieces* of the puzzle of the universe are believed to complete the *whole* puzzle and we tuck the box away in a drawer, no longer puzzling, no longer striving to put together the pieces within our grasp. So ironically, these champions of thought are the ones who think they can stop thinking. However, it often doesn't take long before human history itself shows that many of their puzzle pieces just don't fit.

Scientific materialism had all but solved the puzzle of human society and happiness early in the 20th century. God and religion were merely the "opium of the people," according to Karl Marx — but where are the communists today? They're getting harder to find, even within American universities. And before God was a delusion to Dawkins, he was an illusion to Sigmund Freud. Freud, too, had apparently solved the puzzle of man (with God an imaginary piece of man's own fabrication). The Freudians ruled psychiatry and clinical psychology for decades, but where are they today?

John B. Watson and B. F. Skinner led a scientific revolution in American behavioristic psychology in the 20th century.[3] The mind itself was a fiction that did not matter. Human behavior was conceived to be simply the product of outside forces — chance associations with rewards and punishments. Society, it was argued, need only change the rewards and the punishments to shape individual behaviors to its liking. The behaviorists had little to say about any crucial role for instinct, genes, or evolution. Religion, in their view, was merely superstition arising from chance rewards of superstitious behavior.

The behaviorists surely held some valid pieces of the puzzle. We do learn from associations, and our environments do help shape our beliefs and our behaviors. But we are more than pigeons pecking so as to obtain pellets.

Domestic Chicks

And speaking of pecking, Richard Dawkin's doctoral dissertation was entitled *Selective Pecking in the Domestic Chick*. Though I've not read it, judging from what I've read from his writings on purely biological subject matters, I imagine it's... well... impeccable. I was blessed with the opportunity to do my doctoral research with human beings at a medical school's neuropsychology laboratory, and my dissertation was entitled *Executive Functioning in Early Alzheimer's Disease*.

Now, there is an old saying that if the only tool you've got is a hammer, then everything looks like a nail. Those folks who take materialistic and behavioristic approaches to understanding man use their understanding of lower animals — and now even miniscule parts of animals, such as strands of DNA — to hammer home their points about man. To Skinner, we were merely pigeons with bigger brains; and to Dawkins, we are animated robots designed to carry about our real masters — selfish little genes.

Okay, here's why I'm using the dissertational contrast. When I studied the complex mental abilities of individuals very early in the throes of Alzheimer's dementia, I studied to what extent and in what patterns human beings lose "executive" thinking abilities. These abilities include such things as the capacity to solve complex problems, to reason abstractly, to form concepts, to set and maintain long-term practical goals, to purposefully search and recall memorized information, to express thought in language and in writing, to inhibit reflexive behaviors in keeping with social norms, and to self-reflect and monitor and regulate one's own thinking processes and behaviors. I was testing *uniquely human abilities* that pigeons and chickens and strands of DNA do not possess.

The awareness of these abilities that are absolutely unique to us is not new, of course. Such abilities have always defined us as human, and great thinkers have always been aware of this. Aristotle wrote about them many centuries years ago. And so, unlike the new atheists, he began his analysis of any subject matter by giving credit to the ideas of the great thinkers who came before him. What is relatively new is the denial that these abilities make us any different from the other animals, or that they reflect the way that we were made in the image of God — that is, in possessing intellect and will.

The Spirit of Materialism

Materialistic atheists believe that nothing but matter matters. The new Darwinian atheists in particular are a hard-nosed lot who do not admit the existence of a spiritual realm. They think that if we cannot see it, hear it, taste it, touch it, or smell it, then it does not exist — or that it is a mere by-product, or even delusion, with no significance of its own, such as the "illusion" of human free will or the "delusion" of God. They hold to this idea with obstinate passion. And yet, neither we nor they themselves can see, hear, taste, touch, or smell their idea. How much does a consciousness raised by Darwin weigh, I wonder? What color is it? How loud might it be? If I say that it "stinks" or "leaves a bad taste in my mouth," I'm merely being metaphorical.

When the atheists put "science" and "reason" on pedestals, how unfortunate it is that we can't take photographs of science and reason to hang on our walls to gather inspiration. Of course, science and reason are "things" that exist not as matter, but as the ideas of the human mind. Are they, then, any less real?

Right now, look out your nearest window — it's a flying pig!

I apologize for misleading you, because even though I don't know where you're sitting, I am certain that a flying pig was not sailing by it.[4] Both you and I, however, are able to form this mental image of a flying pig, something we have never seen in nature. Also, by the fact of your human intellect, I'm pretty certain that you "saw" some kind of an image in your "mind's eye" when you read my passage. Our intellects are not strictly material. We can imagine virtually anything.

Also, note how my idea of this imaginary flying porker — this idea itself having no mass, volume, density (well, maybe it was a little "dense"), color, scent, shape, taste or smell (unless perhaps converted to flying hickory-smoked bacon) — has produced an actual effect on your own mental imaging. Of course, as a human being, I chose to express this idea to you using my will, and I had to do it by physical means, using my brain to form my own mental image, my fingers as instruments upon the keyboard, my computer to send this to my editor, and then you had to pick up the book and read the printed page. It's a bit of a complicated process, but that is how we humans operate as mind/body, spirit/matter composites.

But God, you see, is not matter — though you could say in more than one sense that He matters very much. As humans, our ideas and our wills must be made manifest through the instruments of our bodies. God is pure spirit, and His will is made manifest directly, completely, and eternally without complex, material, external means. He did, however, choose to take on flesh and enter into time to reveal himself to us, and I'll get to that in just a minute.

The Spirit of Superman

Human beings are more than merely thinkers, of course. Aristotle noted long ago that man, the uniquely "rational animal," was also a "political animal" — meaning literally in his day, "one who lives in a polis" or a city-state. Today we would emphasize that man is a "social animal" as well. We don't just think abstract thoughts; we feel and we act, and most often in relationships with our family, friends, neighbors, acquaintances, co-workers, and fellow citizens of all sorts. While we need intellectual heroes who can serve as models of clear and penetrating thought, we also need action heroes who can serve as models of kind and just and courageous behaviors in our dealings with our fellow man.

I've already told you that as an American child of the 1960s, I considered myself most blessed in regard to the availability of action heroes. The Superman of the comics and the screen may have borrowed his name from Nietzsche and Shaw, but their "superman" was a most self-absorbed and pitiful little specimen compared to this guy. His powers soared beyond anything found on Earth, but he was by no stretch of the comic writer's imagination "beyond good and evil." Evil was his enemy. He fought for the right. His might did not make things right.

Superman stood for "truth, justice, and the American way," and I think it is safe to say that "the American way" was interpreted at that time to mean the American respect for the fundamental human rights of "life, liberty, and the pursuit of happiness," as proudly proclaimed in our Declaration of Independence. And please recall how the concepts of these fundamental rights were influenced by the natural law theories of the Stoics and St. Thomas Aquinas. Of course, many of these rights are under attack today, but maybe we can draw strength from our own action heroes, whoever they may be, to boldly stand up and defend them.

When Superman was cast as the ideal hero, please note how closely he resembled, not the Nietzschean warrior who would rule and destroy, but a figure of immense power who chooses to serve and to sacrifice. We can certainly do much worse than to draw inspiration from Superman — but we can also do infinitely better!

The Spirit and Flesh of the *Real* Superman

In *Fides et Ratio*, Pope John Paul II brings up a profound connection between what Aristotle would call our rational and our political natures in discussing issues of evidence and belief:

> There are in the life of a human being many more truths which are simply believed than truths which are acquired by way of personal verification. Who, for instance, could assess critically the countless scientific findings upon which modern life is based? Who could personally examine the flow of information which comes day after day from all parts of the world and which is generally accepted as true? ... In believing, we entrust ourselves to the knowledge acquired by other people. This suggests an important tension. On the one hand, the knowledge acquired through belief can seem an imperfect form of knowledge, to be perfected gradually through personal accumulation of evidence; on the other hand, belief is often humanly richer than mere evidence, because it involves an interpersonal relationship and brings into play not only a person's capacity to know but also the deeper capacity to entrust oneself to others, to enter into a relationship with them which is intimate and enduring.[5]

It is also in regard to this interplay between the quest for knowledge and the need to trust and believe in others that

Truth itself became flesh, that we might find truth through our belief in Him. In the words of St. Clement of Alexandria (c. A.D. 150-c. 215), who was a man as immersed in the culture of the ancient Greeks as that of the ancient Christians: "We call philosophers *those who love the wisdom that is creator and mistress of all things, that is knowledge of the Son of God*."[6] In the story of Superman, a superior being came to Earth from a planet far away and devoted himself to helping humanity. In the reality of Jesus Christ, Being Itself took flesh and came to earth, devoting and sacrificing himself to save humanity and to offer eternal bliss. It is ingrained in our nature to seek the truth and to seek to love and be loved. Jesus Christ is the answer to these yearnings. Atheists draw a caricature of Him, as if He were some comic-book creation, yet He is the author of the human nature that allows us all to be inspired by those heroes, comic and otherwise, who strive to use and build their powers, both intellectual and physical, to love and serve their fellow man.

Here, then, is my concluding advice to the would-be atheist — and it is only "my" advice to the extent that I have borrowed from far greater thinkers before me.

Before you give up on Christ and the Church, please make sure you know just who and what you are giving up. Go ahead and read the books of the atheists, both old and new. (My preference is to borrow them from the library, since I'd prefer my coins go to different coffers.) Think carefully about what they say. Then go to your nearest Catholic bookstore or website and obtain some of the modern books that answer them (see again Truth Box #11, p. 181). Also, be sure to read actual writings of the Catholic Church, such as the *Catechism of the Catholic Church*, as well as masterpieces by the greatest thinkers in our heritage, folks like St. Augustine and St. Thomas Aquinas of centuries past, and Pope John Paul II and Pope Benedict XVI of recent and current memory. Bear in mind that Scripture itself calls "the Church of the living God, the pillar and bulwark of the truth" (1 Tim 3:15).

Finally, speaking of Scripture itself, make sure you are acquainted with all four Gospels themselves, the wisdom literature of the Old Testament, the letters of Paul, and the letter of James, at a minimum. Meditate upon your readings, consult the inner light of your conscience, and ask for God's guidance before you make your decision.

And please note well that you need never leave your brains at the door of the Catholic Church. Its intellectual history is rich and unparalleled, gathering in truths from wherever in the world they may be found, and from wherever in heaven and on earth they may be revealed to us. It stands replete with unparalleled stories of love and joyous fulfillment as well.

You need not give up science to obtain religion. You can fly higher with the wing of reason when it moves in rhythm with the wing of faith. Never forget that survival of the fittest pales in comparison with love your neighbor. We were made to think great thoughts and to do great things, within the limits of our natures. We are not Supermen or Wonder Women, but we are indeed superbly and wondrously made. We are made in His image, and we will fulfill ourselves most fully in heart and mind, body and soul, when we attempt to image Him in our thoughts and in our deeds.

Thank you for reading along. Now it's time to move up, up, and away from atheism — and towards the real Superman.

TRUTH BOX #13

The Words of the Word

Jesus said to him, "I am the way, and the truth, and the life; no one comes to the Father, but by me." (Jn 14:6)

Human reason cannot grasp the triune nature of God the Father, God the Son, and God the Holy Spirit, though it can provide some aid in helping us to understand this mystery, within the limits of our intellectual capacities. It has been made known to us through divine revelation, through God's written word, and primarily through the actual incarnated appearance of "The Word," which was present since the beginning with the Father. We must employ faith, as well as reason, to embrace Him.

My parting advice to the would-be atheist, or perhaps to the "would desire to be no longer" atheist, is to study the words of "the Word." Dust off your copy of the New Testament and dig right in to those "red letter" passages of Sts. Matthew, Mark, Luke, and John. See what He who is the Word, the Good Shepherd, the Truth, the Way, the Life, the Door, the Vine, the Bread of Life, the Light of the World, the Savior, and the Lamb of God actually had to say to us. But be sure to read the black texts as well, to see what He taught by His actions and His life.

Jesus was learned and wise. He knew the Hebrew Scriptures better than elder rabbis. He healed the sick, made the blind see, raised the dead, forgave sinners, supped with tax collectors, and withheld the use of His unimaginable power when He suffered, even unto death.

204 | From Atheism to Catholicism

"Greater love has no man than this, that a man lay down his life for his friends" (Jn 15:13). He had this kind of love. We must always remember: If we choose atheism, we reject not only an abstract philosophical opinion; we reject Him.

How much greater is a life devoted to seeking, finding, knowing, imitating, and embracing Him!

An Ode to the Real Superman

What have you done to overcome?
So the bold Nietzscheans say.
The will to pow'r enables some
To hold others in their sway.
But what will humans have become
If true justice goes away?

Superman does not crush others.
He gives his strength to the weak.
Every human is his brother.
"Truth and justice," hear him speak.
He's born of no earthly mother,
He's an image of our peak.

Heroes outlive our childhood dreams,
Men and women need goals, too.
Something to strive for, it seems,
Mankind must never eschew.
We, too, must gain strength from sunbeams,
If we are to grow anew.

One Hero takes us beyond self.
As we strive to grow like Him.
Some would leave His book on the shelf,
And sing to cold matter a hymn.
"He's like Santa Claus, the old elf,
a figment, a dream, a whim."

But He's far more than fairy tale.
The Truth, the Way, and the Light.
Those who know Him will not fail
To get the universe right.
Faith nor Reason will ever pale
When He is within our sight.

Let us grow in humility
And in the love wisdom brings.
Let us let loose ability
To think beyond merely things.
Let us achieve facility
In seeking the King of Kings.

Notes

Foreword: God Bless the Atheists

1. Pope John Paul II, *Fides et Ratio* ("Faith and Reason," 1998 encyclical) (Vatican City: Vatican Publishing House, 1998), n. 48.

2. Walter Kaufmann (ed.), *The Portable Nietzsche* (New York, Penguin Books, 1968), p. 66.

3. Roger Stern, *The Death and Life of Superman* (New York: Bantam Books, 1993).

4. "For the greater glory of God."

Introduction: Neither Bird, nor Plane, but Superman!

1. Kaufmann, *The Portable Nietzsche*, p. 124. Note that Kaufmann actually translates Nietzsche's *ubermench* "overman," rather than the more familiar "superman." The meaning is the same.

2. Heinz L. Ansbacher and Rowena R. Ansbacher (eds.), *The Individual Psychology of Alfred Adler* (New York: Harper & Row, 1956), pp. 103 and 104.

PART I: GOD IS DEAD?

1. Will Durant, *The Story of Philosophy* (New York: Garden City Publishing Co., 1938), p. 451. Nietzsche's work is often referred to as *Thus Spake Zarathustra*.

Chapter 1. Friedrich Nietzsche's Superman

1. Kaufmann, *The Portable Nietzsche*, p. 124.

2. Durant, *The Story of Philosophy*, p. 453.

3. "Scaevola" means essentially "lefty."

4. David Elkind, *All Grown Up and No Place to Go: Teenagers in Crisis*, revised edition (New York: De Capo Press), 1997.

4. Kaufmann, *The Portable Nietzsche*, pp. 103-439.

6. Ibid., p. 103.

7. Ibid., p. 289.

8. Ibid., p. 169

9. Durant, *The Story of Philosophy*, p. 463.

10. I've switched to underlining with colored pencils in recent years, which has led to rather beautifully highlighted volumes of the *Summa Theologica*, which we'll come to in Chapter 9.

11. A favorite of Mentzer, and of Nietzsche himself before he ended his friendship with Wagner because the composer's music became too "Christian."

12. A phrase I picked up from Mentzer — and I still do like my coffee that way!

13. Aristotle wrote of an ideal man he called the "magnanimous" or "great-souled" man in his *Nicomachean Ethics*, whose manly virtue was guided by the "golden mean" — by balance, moderation, and "nothing in excess." Nietzsche considered this a degradation of older Greek warrior values, which helped pave the way for Christian ethical ideals.

14. But please note as well that some have come to overemphasize this fact. As we will see in the chapters to come on Ellis, Adler, and the Stoics, we must not overlook the power of the conscious to temper the unconscious, and of purposeful goals to redirect instinctual drives.

15. Kaufmann, *The Portable Nietzsche*, p. 576. Emphasis in original.

Chapter 2. The Lord and Lord Bertrand Russell

1. Bertrand Russell, *Why I Am Not a Christian* (New York: Simon & Schuster, 1957), p. 56.

2. Ibid., p. 30.

3. *Time*, Vol. XVI, No. 14 (Oct. 6, 1930).

4. St. Thomas Aquinas, *Summa Theologica* (Notre Dame, IN: Christian Classics, 1991), *II-II, Q. 27*, p. 1299.

5. Ibid., II-II, Q. 32, a.5, p. 1321.

6. Ibid., II-II, Q. 58, a.1, p. 1429.

7. Robert E. Egner and Lester E. Denonn (eds.), *The Basic Writings of Bertrand Russell* (New York: Simon & Schuster, 1961), p. 353.

8. Ibid., p. 82.

9. Russell, *Why I Am Not a Christian*, p. 46.

10. Bertrand Russell, *The Conquest of Happiness* (New York: W.W. Norton & Co. Inc., 1996), p. 54.

11. Ibid., p. 54.

12. Ibid., p. 56.

13. Ibid., p. 47.

14. Ibid., p. 69.

15. Ibid., p. 153.

16. Russell, *Why I Am Not a Christian*, p. 24.

Chapter 3. Albert Ellis: Reason, Emotion, Psychotherapy, and Jehovah

1. Albert Ellis, *Rational Emotive Behavior Therapy: It Works for Me — It Can Work for You* (New York: Prometheus Books, 2004), p. 114. Emphasis in original.

2. Ibid., p. 193. (Ellis himself is, of course, the "St. Albert" to whom he refers.)

3. Albert Ellis, *Reason and Emotion in Psychotherapy: A Comprehensive Method of Treating Human Disturbance*, revised and updated (New York: Birch Lane Press, 1994), p. 106.

4. Ibid., p. 34.

5. Charles Murray, *Human Accomplishment: The Pursuit of Excellence in the Arts and Sciences, 800 B.C. to 1950* (New York: Harper Collins, 2003).

6. Ellis, *Reason and Emotion in Psychotherapy*, pp. 107-116. These beliefs are all extensively described throughout the book.

7. Ellis, *Rational Emotive Behavior Therapy*, p. 114.

8. Ibid., p. 117.

9. Ibid., p. 118.

10. Ibid., p. 114.

Chapter 4. Aristotle Shrugged: Ayn Rand and the Intellectual Soul

1. From "Galt's Speech" in *Atlas Shrugged*, reproduced in Ayn Rand, *For the New Intellectual: The Philosophy of Ayn Rand* (New York: Random House, 1961), p. 191.

2. Ibid., pp. 178-179.

3. Ayn Rand, *The Fountainhead* (New York: Signet, 1971), p. ix.

4. Rand saw this damning, or "blaming the good for being good," in practices like progressive taxation of the rich, which she saw as a penalty or punishment for achievements that benefit oneself and mankind.

5. Readers familiar with the book will recall that question as one of the taglines that appears again and again throughout the novel itself.

6. Have you ever seen the movie *High Noon*, starring Gary Cooper? Can you guess who played Roark in Hollywood's version of *The Fountainhead*? Yes, it was Gary Cooper.

7. I can't help but wonder what Rand might think about the depths to which popular media and pop culture have sunk since her own death in 1982.

8. From "Galt's Speech" in *Atlas Shrugged*, reproduced in Ayn Rand, *For the New Intellectual*, p. 152.

Chapter 5. Darwin and Dawkins: Genes, Memes, and "Me's"

1. Charles Darwin, *On the Origin of Species by Means of Natural Selection* (New York: Random House, 1979), p. 458.

2. Richard Dawkins, *The God Delusion* (New York: Mariner Books, 2008), p. 232.

3. *http://richarddawkins.net/article,2025,THE-FOUR-HORSEMEN, Discussions-With-Richard-Dawkins-Episode-1-RDFRS*.

4. Darwin, *On the Origin of Species by Means of Natural Selection*, p. 65.

5. Ibid., p. 458.

6. Ibid., p. 460.

7. Ibid., p. 458.

8. Ibid., p. 459.

9. Ellis, *Rational Emotive Behavior Therapy*, p. 114.

10. Cited in Alister McGrath, *Dawkin's God: Genes, Memes, and the Meaning of Life* (Malden, MA: Blackwell Publishing, 2007), p. 84.

11. Dawkins, *The God Delusion*, p. 57.

12. Ibid., p. 74.

13. James W. Fowler, *Stages of Faith: The Psychology of Human Development* (New York: HarperOne, 1995).

14. Dawkins, *The God Delusion*, p. 74.

15. Ibid., p. 76.

16. Must reality itself be so "toothy" and vicious? Perhaps it must be when "I believe in the survival of the fittest" begins one's creed of faith.

17. Dawkins, *The God Delusion*, p. 175.

18. Ibid., p. 175.

19. Ibid., p. 221.

20. St. Thomas Aquinas, *Summa Theologica*, II-II, Q.2, a.10, p. 1181.

21. Ibid., *I-I, Q. 85, a.7*, p. 439.

22. Dawkins, *The God Delusion*, p. 195.

23. Ibid., p. 129.

24. Kevin Vost, *Book Review: The International Handbook of Giftedness and Talent* (second edition), *Mensa Research Journal*, Winter 2002 (Vol. 33, No. 1), pp. 91-93.

25. Susan Blackmore, *The Meme Machine* (New York: Oxford University Press, 2000).

26. Dawkins, *The God Delusion*, p. 228.

27. Religious education of the young is something that Richard Dawkins himself vehemently opposes as "child abuse" in *The God Delusion*.

Part II: Signs of Life

1. Seneca, *Letters from a Stoic* (New York: Penguin Books, 1969), p. 162.

Chapter 6. Alfred Adler and the Fictive Goal of God

1. Ansbacher, *The Individual Psychology of Alfred Adler*, p. 176.

2. Ibid. p. 461.

3. Ibid., p. 136.

4. Caesar's words are often reported in his native Latin as *"Alea iacta est,"* but Caesar was quoting a line from an ancient Greek play.

5. William Shakespeare, *Julius Caesar*, I, ii, 140-141.

6. Ansbacher, *The Individual Psychology of Alfred Adler*, p. 460.

7. Alfred Adler, *Superiority and Social Interest* (New York: W.W. Norton & Co. Inc., 1979), p. 286.

8. Ibid., p. 277.

9. Lee Strobel, *The Case for a Creator: A Journalist Investigates Scientific Evidence That Points Toward God* (Grand Rapids, MI: Zondervan, 2004).

Chapter 7. Stoic Strivings: The Slave, the Lawyer, the Emperor, and God

1. Seneca, *Letters from a Stoic*, p. 103.

2. Mark Forstater, *The Spiritual Teachings of Marcus Aurelius* (New York: HarperCollins, 2000), p. 203.

3. Epictetus, *Discourses* (Cambridge, MA: Harvard University Press, 2000), p. 111.

4. Seneca, *Letters from a Stoic*, Letter II, p. 34.

5. Ibid., Letter V, p. 37.

6. Ibid., Letter V, p. 37.

7. Ibid., Letter VI, p. 39.

8. Ibid., Letter VI, p. 40.

9. Ibid., Letter XI, p. 56.

10. Seneca, *Moral Essays*, vol. 2, *On the Shortness of Life* vii, 3 (Cambridge, MA: Harvard University Press), p. 305.

11. Marcus Aurelius, *Meditations* (Cambridge, MA: Harvard University Press, 2003), pp. 7-9.

12. Ibid., p. 17.

13. Ibid., p. 3.

14. Ibid., p. 9.

15. Ibid., p. 27.

16. Epictetus, *The Enchiridion* (Cambridge, MA: Harvard University Press, 2000), p. 487.

17. Ibid., p. 483.

18. Epictetus, *The Discourses*, Books III-IV (Cambridge, MA: Harvard University Press, 2000), p. 125.

19. Ibid., p. vii.

Chapter 8. Mortimer Adler and the God of the Philosophers

1. Mortimer Adler, *Truth in Religion: The Plurality of Religions and the Unity of Truth* (New York: Macmillan, 1990), p. 15. Emphasis in original.

2. Ibid., p. 92.

3. Mortimer J. Adler, *How to Think About God: A Guide for the 20th-Century Pagan* (New York: Macmillan, 1980), p. 165.

4. Alan Sokal and Jean Bricmont, *Fashionable Nonsense: Postmodern Intellectuals' Abuse of Science* (New York: Picador Books, 1998).

5. Mortimer J. Adler, *Aristotle for Everybody: Difficult Thought Made Easy* (New York: Macmillan, 1978).

6. Mortimer J. Adler, *How to Read a Book: The Art of Getting a Liberal Education* (New York: Simon & Schuster, 1940).

7. Adler, *How to Think About God*, p. 6.

8. Ibid., p. 144. Emphasis in original.

9. Ibid., p. 146.

10. Ibid., p. 167.

11. Mortimer Adler, *The Difference of Man and the Difference It Makes* (New York: Fordham University Press, 1993).

12. Antony Flew, *There Is a God: How the World's Most Notorious Atheist Changed His Mind* (New York: HarperOne, 2007).

13. Ibid., p. 93.

14. Ibid., p. 157.

Part III: Christ Has Risen From His Tomb!

1. St. Thomas Aquinas, *Summa Contra Gentiles* (Notre Dame, IN: University of Notre Dame Press, 1975).

Chapter 9. St. Thomas Aquinas:
The Angelic Doctor Effects a Cure

1. Pope Leo XIII, *Aeterni Patris* (1879 encyclical on the restoration of Christian philosophy), in St. Thomas Aquinas, *Summa Theologica* (Notre Dame, IN: Christian Classics, 1991), p. xvii.

2. Pope Pius XI, *Studiorum Ducem* (1923 encyclical on St. Thomas Aquinas) (Vatican City: Vatican Publishing House, 1923), n. 28.

3. Pope John Paul II, *Fides et Ratio*, n. 47.

4. Ibid., n. 61.

5. Frances A. Yates, *The Art of Memory* (Chicago: University of Chicago Press, 1974), p. 82.

6. Pope Leo XIII, *Aeterni Patris*, in *Summa Theologica*, p. xv.

7. C. S. Lewis, *Mere Christianity* (New York: Touchstone, 1996), p. 148.

8. Dawkins, *The God Delusion*, p. 285.

9. Seneca, *Letters from a Stoic*, Letter XI, p. 56.

10. St. Thomas Aquinas, *Summa Theologica*, II-II, Q.2, a.10, p. 1181.

11. Victor J. Stenger, *God: The Failed Hypothesis: How Science Shows That God Does Not Exist* (Amherst, NY: Prometheus Books, 2007).

12. Christopher Hitchens, *God Is Not Great: How Religion Poisons Everything* (New York: Hachette Book Group, 2008).

Chapter 10. C. S. Lewis: God Save the Queen

1. C. S. Lewis, *Mere Christianity*, p. 45.

2. Ibid., p. 47

3. Ibid., p. 75.

4. Ibid., p. 54.

5. Ibid.

214 | From Atheism to Catholicism

6. Ibid., p. 55.

7. Ibid., p. 54.

8. To a state of lighthearted enjoyment — a phrase attributed to St. Thomas Aquinas.

9. Virgil, *Aeneid* (Cambridge, MA: Harvard University Press, 2000), p. 263.

10. Lewis, *Mere Christianity*, p. 56.

11. Dawkins, *The God Delusion*, p. 117.

12. C. S. Lewis, *The Chronicles of Narnia* (New York: HarperCollins, 1994), p. 146.

Chapter 11. G. K. Chesterton:
What Could Be Right With the World

1. G. K. Chesterton, *What's Wrong With the World* (San Francisco: Ignatius Press, 1994), p. 37.

2. G. K. Chesterton, *The Catholic Church and Conversion* (San Francisco: Ignatius Press, 2006), p. 48.

3. Ibid., p. 74.

4. Ibid., p. 70.

5. From "The Debate with Bertrand Russell," *BBC Magazine* (11/27/35), cited at *http://www.whatswrongwiththeworld.net/2009/06/anniversary_of_g_k_chestertons.html*.

6. *http://en.wikipedia.org/wiki/G._K._Chesterton#cite_note-10*.

7. See Richard Dawkins, *Climbing Mount Improbable* (New York: Norton Co., 1997), pp. 266-268.

8. G. K. Chesterton, *Orthodoxy* (San Francisco: Ignatius Press, 1995), pp. 65-66.

9. Ibid., p. 25.

10. Ibid., pp. 23-24.

11. See Lewis, *Mere Christianity*, p. 11.

12. See G. K. Chesterton, *Orthodoxy*, p. 17.

13. Margaret Sanger is cited as a great "hero" on Planned Parenthood's current website's "History & Successes" section. Among Sanger's *bon mots* is this brief commentary on the effects of public charity in the early 20th century: "We are now in a state where our charities, our compensation acts, our pensions, hospitals, and even our drainage and sanitation equipment all tend to keep alive the sickly and the weak, who are allowed to propagate and in turn produce a race of degenerates" ("Birth

Control and Women's Health," *Birth Control Review*, Vol. 1, No. 12 [December 1917], p. 7). Cited in Donald De Marco and Benjamin Wiker, *Architects of the Culture of Death* (San Francisco: Ignatius Press, 2004), p. 297.

14. *http://davidszondy.com/future/man/chesterton.htm*.

Chapter 12. Pope John Paul II:
Faith and Reason, Body and Soul

1. Pope John Paul II, *Fides et Ratio*, Preamble.

2. Ibid., n. 18.

3. Ibid., n. 34.

4. Ibid., n. 28.

5. Ibid., n. 46.

6. Ibid., n. 55.

7. Ibid., n. 55.

8. Indeed, it was just such a matchup that made for a great dramatic movie, *Inherit the Wind*, based on the Scopes "Monkey" Trial of 1925, in which renowned lawyer Clarence Darrow defended teacher John Scopes, who was arrested for violating a Tennessee state law that prohibited the teaching of evolution in public schools. The old version (1960), with Spencer Tracy playing the defense attorney, is my favorite.

9. Cited in Christoph Cardinal Schönborn, *Creation and Evolution: A Conference with Pope Benedict XVI in Castel Gandolfo* (San Francisco: Ignatius Press, 2008), p. 91.

Conclusion: The Real Superman

1. Pope John Paul II, *Fides et Ratio*, n. 34.

2. That first great commandment is: "You shall love the Lord your God with all your heart, and with all your soul, and with all your mind, and with all your strength" (Mk 12:30).

3. One of Watson's claims to fame was a notorious experiment in which a young child was taught to fear rabbits. Skinner was famous for explaining human behavior based largely on his research with pigeons.

4. Richard Dawkins and Albert Ellis would disagree with me on this one. You see, in their view, I could not say that I was certain a flying pig was not sailing past your window, only that it was highly improbable, perhaps to the order of a .000000001 percent chance. And speaking of flying livestock, in Louis de Wohl's *The Quiet Light: A Novel*

about Saint Thomas Aquinas (Philadelphia and New York: J. B. Lippin-cott, 1950), fellow friars yell for Thomas to come to the window to see a flying ox. When they laugh at Thomas for coming to the window, his retort was: "I'd rather believe that an ox can fly than that a Dominican could lie" (p. 199).

5. Pope John Paul II, *Fides et Ratio*, nn. 31-32.

6. Ibid., n. 38. Emphasis added.

Notes

Notes

Notes

Notes

Notes

Notes